hope
when
your
heart
is
heavy

Table of Contents

Does that hard thing you're walking through make you question if God sees everyone else's pain but yours?

Heartbreak. Disappointment. Discouragement. Uncertainties of the future. Hopelessness.

Unfortunately, these are emotions countless people struggle with every single day as a result of challenging circumstances of life that, over time, leave us feeling full of anxiety, void of peace and grasping for any glimpse of hope.

With so many challenges to face and the never-ending barrage of life's hardships, it can become hard to believe better times are on the horizon. The longer we pray for God's intervention yet see nothing happening, the more likely we are to start feeling hopeless and wondering if God really sees or even cares about what we're going through. We may even begin to doubt if His promises of hope, peace, comfort and rest — promises our souls desperately long for — are really possible for us.

Hopelessness is not a new emotion. Every generation since the creation of the world has experienced difficult times that have left God's people feeling exhausted and despondent about the future. Isaiah knew the desperate need to hope in something worthy of hope. So he spoke these words: *"but those who hope in the LORD will renew their strength. They will soar on wings like eagles; they will run and not grow weary, they will walk and not be faint"* (Isaiah 40:31, NIV).

Isaiah shared this encouragement with the Israelites who had been exiled in Babylon for decades. They had come to the conclusion that God must not care about them and that their troubles would never end, leaving them feeling defeated, discouraged and overcome with hopelessness.

Just like the Israelites, who were weak in body and spirit, we, too, can reach the point of complete emotional and physical exhaustion, opening the door for hopelessness to invade our thoughts and steal any ounce of joy we ever felt. Isaiah knew that only in God's strength can we continue pushing forward during the hardest of times and trust Him with the details of our lives while we wait for His sovereign plans to play out — plans we may not understand at all.

Maybe today you are weak in body and spirit. Maybe peace seems like a promise out of reach, meant for everyone else but you. Maybe hopelessness has taken up residence in your heart for so long you wonder if you can make it another day.

If this describes you, sweet friend, this book was written for you.

It is our prayer at Proverbs 31 Ministries that God's comfort, peace and hope will sink deep into your heart with each devotion you read in this book. We pray you are filled with a renewed peace, knowing that God has you, your circumstances and your future in His sovereign care and that His plans are always good.

Each of these comforting and uplifting devotions was written by a member of COMPEL Training, Proverbs 31 Ministries' online writers training program. These women, like you, have experienced difficulties, adversities, times of doubt and hopelessness, yet they have also witnessed God's protection and love and are now passionate about spreading that same hope to those who need it most.

It is our prayer this book encourages you to fix your eyes on Jesus and trust He has your present circumstances and your future in His hands. We pray the words you read will breathe new life and renewed hope into every weary soul.

HOPE
IN THE
MIDST OF
UNMET
EXPECTATIONS

When the Road You Are Traveling Doesn't Lead You Home

SANDELL SNYDER

"... fix our eyes not on what is seen, but on what is unseen, since what is seen is temporary, but what is unseen is eternal." 2 Corinthians 4:18 (NIV)

I could no longer ignore the heartbreaking reality: The path of my life would not lead to the place I imagined. I always assumed my adult life would reside in marriage and motherhood. There was nothing I anticipated more. But the mother part didn't happen.

The hole this created in my life, in my heart, was more than disappointment. It was a dream denied, and it left me wandering in the wilderness for a long, long time. The reality was like standing on the edge of a cliff, looking over an impassable canyon into a land, a life, that would never be mine, and feeling so very ... rejected ... isolated ... confused.

I was grieving the loss of purpose and place. This turmoil drew me to the story of Moses in Deuteronomy. He, too, faced a hard reality, standing on a mountain, looking from a distance into a place he would never go. Called by God to lead the Israelites out of bondage, Moses spent decades face to face with God as they journeyed from Egypt to the promised land. Of course Moses expected to enter into that land. But it didn't happen.

If Moses' story ended there, I might have remained stranded on that cliff, aching for the fulfillment lost by entry denied. But centuries after the Exodus, the Gospels record Moses talking with Jesus on another mountaintop. (Luke 9:30)

You see, when Moses passed through physical death, his story didn't end. Like the tabernacle in the desert and the temple in Jerusalem, the land of Canaan was a temporary, imperfect stand-in for the divine destination awaiting God's people.

Moses wasn't denied entry to the place that his heart desired; his journey simply bypassed the earthly model and led him straight into the true promised land — eternity with Jesus.

I found such hope in this realization. It was never about land or even milk and honey. It was always about God leading His people home to Him.

Sure, Moses was disappointed that he would not cross the Jordan, but he wasn't wrecked by it. His relationship with God wasn't about arriving or doing — it was about living with God. He didn't get lost looking for purpose or place because he found both of those in God's radiant face.

So often, our eyes and hearts mistake counterfeits as the objects of our longings, and we forget to look to the kingdom beyond, the place we truly belong. We forget that our identity and hope is in God alone, not in something we do or become. But the Apostle Paul reminds us not to lose heart but instead to *"... fix our eyes not on what is seen, but on what is unseen, since what is seen is temporary, but what is unseen is eternal"* (2 Corinthians 4:18).

No, the paths of our lives may not lead to the places we imagine, but if we focus our gaze on God's face, our journey will take us to a much greater place.

An Empty Carriage and a Hope–Filled Heart

KIMBERLY JABBAR

"Delight yourself in the LORD and he will give you the desires of your heart." Psalm 37:4 (NIV, 1988)

"Please let there be a line," I silently pleaded.

It had been a long three years of trying to get pregnant. In those same three years, one friend got pregnant and delivered her sixth child! Another gave birth to her first and second children. As my heart celebrated with them, it ached for me.

No line. My season of barrenness continued. Perhaps you can relate. Something good you want so badly and yet, for now, the answer is no.

No child.
No spouse.
No addiction-free loved one.
No healthy diagnosis.
No promotion.

Thankfully, in my time of disappointment, I found hope and life-changing direction in Psalm 37:4, which says, *"Delight yourself in the LORD and he will give you the desires of your heart."*

As I chose to focus on the Lord and delight in Him, I noticed my desire for a child shifted. Yes, I still wanted to be a mom with every fiber of my being. But more than I wanted to be a mom, I wanted to learn how to delight myself in Him, especially when things didn't go as expected.

I stopped buying pregnancy tests. I pleaded with God to give me more of Him. And I noticed a shift, not a seismic one but a steadying one. Instead of experiencing a roller coaster of emotions with each passing month, I experienced hope.

God-directed, Spirit-fueled hope. A trusting expectation that was dependent not on my circumstances but on my God. I experienced the hope of Romans 15:13 — *"May the God of **hope** fill you with all joy and peace as you trust in him, so that you may overflow with **hope** by the power of the Holy Spirit"* (NIV, emphasis added).

When we delight in God, the giver of hope, and choose to receive hope from His ever-present Spirit within us, we are filled with joy and peace.

So I delighted in His Word every morning and meditated on it throughout the day rather than fixating on my circumstances. It was often the right verse at the right time. (Psalm 1:2)

I delighted in the Lord, listening only to praise and worship music. It was often the right song at the right time. (Isaiah 61:10)

And through the years, I have learned to delight in my weaknesses, in hardships, in difficulties. Because when I am weak, He is strong. (2 Corinthians 12:10)

I am grateful my period of barrenness took me on a journey that opened the doorway to delighting in Him. Even though I had an empty carriage, I had a hope-filled heart.

While I did eventually have children, it was in the painful waiting that God taught me hope despite my circumstances. I've learned no matter what I face, delighting in Christ is the secret to lasting hope, joy and peace.

Nothing Is Too Hard for God

CAROL WHITAKER

"In hope against hope he believed, so that he might become a father of many nations according to that which had been spoken, 'SO SHALL YOUR DESCENDANTS BE.'" Romans 4:18 (NASB)

I don't believe anymore.

The thought hovered in my mind as I sat on the church pew. I wanted to accept the words and let them stay, although I knew that I shouldn't. God had given me a promise to be used in music long ago. However, I hadn't anticipated the wait would be so long and the trials so many. I felt like giving up and not believing any longer.

As I sat there, I remembered that many months prior I had counseled a friend struggling to believe in God's promise of a child to her. I had so confidently encouraged her to never stop believing. Yet now, due to my circumstances, I wallowed in a similar state of hopelessness and unbelief.

The pastor interrupted my thoughts with an announcement of his theme of "hope" for the message series and "expectant hope" as a theme for the entire year. (I shouldn't have been surprised, but I was!) He then read the following words: *"In hope against hope [Abraham] believed, so that he might become a father of many nations according to that which had been spoken, 'SO SHALL YOUR DESCENDANTS BE'"* (Romans 4:18).

As I learned from the pastor's words and my own research later, the phrase to "hope against hope" is to hold on to hope when we have no grounds for doing so. Generally, when we hope for something, we have a reason to believe we might get whatever we're hoping for. However, to "hope against hope" as mentioned in this passage is to have absolutely no reason to believe it will happen. It is hope that is based entirely on the faithfulness of God.

Abraham believed he would become the father of many nations because of what God had spoken to him. Nothing in his circumstances pointed to this outcome. In fact, everything in his circumstances pointed to a different outcome. Abraham's body, as we learn later in the passage, was as *"good as dead"* and his wife was barren and past childbearing years (Romans 4:19). How could an entire nation come from this old, childless pair?

Simply put, God didn't need perfect circumstances to work. He could do for them what they couldn't do for themselves.

Since looking into the verse, I've been lifted in my spirit. While I have not yet seen the fulfillment of the promise I am praying for, I can cling to the Truth that God will do for me what He has said He will do, even if I can't see how that will happen in the moment.

Wherever we find ourselves, if surveying a situation devoid of hope, we can remember Abraham's situation and the promise he received. Nothing is too hard for God. All that may prevent us in the natural from receiving God's promises will serve to point to His power when He makes a promise come true in spite of the odds stacked against us. And that should infuse us with hope — no matter our circumstance!

Digging Up the Dirt on God

ALLISON DELAGRANGE

"Jesus Christ is the same yesterday and today and forever." Hebrews 13:8 (ESV)

My heart dropped into my stomach. Never in a million years had I seen this coming.

I'd been tossing and turning in bed, finally surrendering to a sleepless night. I groggily reached for my phone for some mindless social media scrolling. When an image of an old friend crossed my screen, my foggy brain jolted into consciousness. This friend was announcing that he was leaving his faith and his church. The truth barreled toward me like a semitruck tearing through a foggy night at full speed. Someone who'd passionately followed Jesus was now walking away into a different lifestyle. This was not what I expected.

I wish I could say I immediately cried out to Jesus. Instead, I got stuck in the intersection of disappointment and curiosity. I'm embarrassed to admit I went digging for dirt on the situation. I became a social media Sherlock Holmes, ready to uncover the pieces of this mystery. At the same time, I mourned how a fellow believer could change so drastically.

Eventually, my search for answers became a quest for hope. Not just because of this circumstance but because of what it represented: Life is full of unmet expectations. Friends may fall away from their faith. Spouses may stray. Mentors may let us down. Where is the hope?

In times like these, the Holy Spirit reminds me of the singular hope on which my life must be built: Jesus Christ Himself. Hebrews 13:8 promises, *"Jesus Christ is the same yesterday and today and forever."* The same God who gave sight to the blind, who turned water into wine and who gave Himself for us is with us today. He is our hope!

It makes me chuckle to think of it this way, but imagine if God had a social media account. His status updates might read:

"Still faithful." (Hebrews 10:23)
"Still righteous." (Psalm 97:2)
"Still loving." (Hosea 3:1)
"Still your source of hope." (Romans 15:13)

I think God would welcome our social media snooping on His page. In fact, what if God is waiting for us to spend time digging up the dirt on Him — praying, listening, studying His Word — so He can show us firsthand that He never fails? What if our greatest letdowns are God's invitation to a deeper relationship with Him, the One who knows what we need before we ask?

Friend, if you're discouraged, envision Jesus standing in the gap between your expectations and reality. Grab His outstretched hand. Sit quietly with Him. Study His Word. Dig up the dirt on God. You'll find fertile soil where your faith can take root and where hope will blossom.

When Hope Is Lost

KELLY BURNS

"Now may the God of hope fill you with all joy and peace in believing, that you may abound in hope by the power of the Holy Spirit." Romans 15:13 (NKJV)

I watched the scene before me, all else a background blur. A young couple with small boys was leaving the birthday party I was attending with my own two small children. The dad swung the youngest of the two boys effortlessly onto his shoulders while grabbing on securely to the waiting hand of the older boy. It was perfect.

And as tears rose up from the deep places of my sadness, choking me … I was reminded that this "perfect" story was not my story. At all. I turned from the scene, blinking back tears and fighting to release the tension in my chest. Like every other event, I would leave this party alone with my children. And there would be no firm hand for them to hold or waiting shoulder to sit upon.

As a little girl playing with dolls, I imagined my future. I knew what was supposed to happen. But that didn't happen for me. And if you would have told me back then what my life would look like, I would have put the dolls back into their case and cried bitter tears.

In truth, "hope" had become an unwelcome word to me. Why? Because I didn't believe in it anymore.

So how do we hope in a God who doesn't seem to care about our dreams? A God who allows our children to be the only ones at the party without a daddy to snuggle them up safely into his arms for the ride home? How do we hope at all? The answer is simple. We can't. Our hearts are too broken. Our dreams are too shattered. Our loss is too heavy.

And so when I read the first words of this passage, my eyes fill with grateful tears:

"Now may the God of hope fill you with all joy and peace in believing, that you may abound in hope by the power of the Holy Spirit" (Romans 15:13).

The God of hope will fill us! God does the filling! This isn't something I could ever do for myself. And do you know what? All these years later, my two small children have grown, and I've discovered something I never made a plan for: Jesus is the One with the firm hand and the waiting shoulders.

And He was all along. Something deep inside of me changed. My vision shifted. And I knew something I hadn't before: His love carried me. It protected me. And it never left us. As daughters of God, we can have hope always … in every moment. In every circumstance. In every heartache. We can have hope … because He is our hope.

Whose Voice Will You Believe?

PERCIS MADDELA

"And say to him, 'Be careful, be quiet, do not fear, and do not let your heart be faint because of these two smoldering stumps of firebrands, at the fierce anger of Rezin and Syria and the son of Remaliah.'" Isaiah 7:4 (ESV)

Not too long ago, I found myself ruminating on all the things I felt God had abandoned in my life.

As a 30-something, I looked at pages of journaled prayers and wondered why I spent time writing out prayers for a godly husband that I didn't yet have. The Post-its on my bedroom wall reminded me of my exhausting fight with obsessive-compulsive disorder. My hands, covered in red, burning and itchy rashes, reminded me of my incurable autoimmune disorder.

Why do I have to experience all this pain and suffering while others around me seem to have it all handed to them? All these things weighed heavily on me, and I began to sink into hopelessness, bitterness and despair. Where was God in all of this?

In today's verse, we learn of someone else who felt overwhelmed and alone. Isaiah 7 tells the story of Ahaz, king of Judah, trembling with fear at a planned military attack by the joined forces of Syria and Israel. Their objective was to get rid of King Ahaz and claim Judah. God directed the prophet Isaiah to speak to King Ahaz. The four things God communicated through Isaiah are: *"Be careful, be quiet, do not fear, and do not let your heart be faint ..."* (Isaiah 7:4).

God wanted King Ahaz to know He was aware of the threats, and He knew Ahaz's fear. God was clearly showing His power and sovereignty over this great force coming against Judah.

In a way, like King Ahaz, I felt surrounded by an insurmountable army of suffering that was planning to take me out, with no way of recovering. I was feasting on the lies of the enemy instead of on God's unfailing Word. It was easier to believe there was nothing good left for me than to believe that God's plan for me was immeasurably more than what I could imagine.

Through a conversation with my cousins, my lack of faith was revealed. I realized I did not believe God or take Him at His word. My cousins also affirmed my struggle by saying, "Percis, you've been through a lot." I felt as if a weight was lifted from my chest. It was my choice who I would believe: myself or God. Choosing God would mean: 1.) believing He has a plan for my struggle and will accomplish His will in my life, and 2.) repenting of believing the wrong voices in my life when I chose unbelief. I repented of it all.

The bitter root was pulled out, and the pain of feeling forgotten went with it. I look back and thank God for bringing me out of that dark valley I was in. All because He told me to believe Him.

Friend, we have a choice today. Regardless of the armies surrounding us, we can choose who we will listen to. It's time to share our pain with others, pray for awareness of lies we've believed, and repent of anything that does not match up with the Lord's calling over us. You're not alone in your struggle. God sees, and He says, *"Be careful, be quiet, do not fear, and do not let your heart be faint ..."* (Isaiah 7:4).

Finding Hope in the Waiting

SUSAN MCALINDEN

"And I will lead the blind in a way that they do not know, in paths that they have not known I will guide them. I will turn the darkness before them into light, the rough places into level ground. These are the things I do, and I do not forsake them." Isaiah 42:16 (ESV)

Nothing was going according to plan! Three years earlier, I reluctantly agreed to move away from our home with our four young children to support my husband's desire to work overseas. Due to unexpected circumstances, our temporary assignment became permanent and we were stranded in a foreign country.

Have you ever found yourself living in circumstances that don't match your expectations? Maybe you are facing an unforeseen health issue, a rocky marriage, infertility or unmet parenting desires. You have done everything in your power to fix the problem, but for every roadblock you move aside, another one appears. You're starting to lose hope, and with a sinking feeling in your spirit, you're wondering if God has a different plan than what your heart desires.

It's hard to pursue an expectation when it feels as if God wants to write an alternative story. How can you hold on to hope when the outcome might break your heart?

I faced this difficult juggling act when we learned that our way home might require moving to a different state, which wasn't home at all.

The only hope I had was to welcome God into my waiting. Every day, I invited Him to join me while I struggled, and I gave Him an earful about my expectations. Daily, He patiently listened ... until one day He spoke. He led me to Isaiah 42:16. This verse says: *"And I will lead the blind in a way that they do not know, in paths that they have not known I will guide them. I will turn the darkness before them into light, the rough places into level ground. These are the things I do, and I do not forsake them."*

The first half of this verse seemed to indicate that my desires for my life would not be met; however, God drew my attention to the verses following those. He will turn the darkness into light, make the rough places smooth and never forsake me.

I'm focused on my expectations because I think I know what's best in my life. However, can I truly find contentment outside of God's will for me?

Instead of searching for hope in the middle of my unmet expectations, maybe I will find peace by accepting His invitation.

We moved to a different state, but His Word was true. Life was full of light. Our paths were remarkably smooth, and He was so very present. We made lifelong friends and many happy memories. And when we least expected it, God moved us back home.

When wrestling with unmet expectations, we all have a choice to make. Do we want to hold on to our unfulfilled aspirations or hand them over to the One who created the desires in our heart? To find the hope you've been wanting, welcome God into your waiting. Don't be afraid to wrestle with your longing. He has a story for you that drives out the darkness, leads you on smooth paths and includes His presence.

Expectant Hope Waits at the Intersection of Longing and Need

KC EDMUNDS

"'But that you may know that the Son of Man has the authority on earth to forgive sins' — he said to the man who was paralyzed — 'I say to you, rise, pick up your bed and go home.'" Luke 5:24 (ESV)

This past year, I suffered a kind of spiritual paralysis. Loneliness and loss seeped into the cracks of my soul, leaving me hopeless, immobile and numb. I sought solace in the typical 21st-century Novocain: scrolling, binge watching, posting — all providing temporary distraction from the pain yet leaving me more distressed and confused.

In today's verse, Jesus' choice to first forgive sin before healing the body inspired a closer look at this well-known account of four faithful men dropping their paralyzed friend through the roof of a packed-out home where He was teaching. Scholars often emphasize faith as a primary theme, and Jesus was certainly moved by their faith, yet He spoke to something deeper.

I never quite understood why Jesus told a man aching for a new body that his sins were forgiven. However, I wonder if Jesus was not only making a statement about His ultimate authority on earth but also relieving a deeper paralysis of the man's soul.

In the passage, Jesus demonstrates He not only sees obvious felt longings but also the deeper, hidden needs of the soul. When I come to Him with a disparity between what feels like my greatest longing and a deeper, unknown need of my soul, He wisely tends to my soul need first, just as He knew what the immobile man on the mat most needed.

This new perspective provides hope, for I know if I miss the mark, Jesus will see the most intimate, aching, sometimes incommunicable needs of my heart. But soul probing is hard work; the things we uncover can be painful. I know because fear had a stranglehold on me for years — and still does at times. When my fears get the better of me, I long for relief. In my ill-defined appeals for freedom, He wisely sees the deeper soul needs to attend to first. If He soothed my fear before helping me address these needs, I would remain less than whole.

Jesus understands how unperceived needs — heart wounds, unforgiveness, bitterness — can strangle the heart, distort the thinking and suffocate the soul. He is keenly aware of body and soul while I can but view the horizon of my immediate circumstances.

HOPE DURING HARD SEASONS

In the Midst of the Storms

AMBER O'BRIEN

"The LORD your God in your midst, the Mighty One, will save; He will rejoice over you with gladness, He will quiet you with His love, He will rejoice over you with singing." Zephaniah 3:17 (NKJV)

So. Much. Rain.

For two whole weeks — long, dark days of rain; short, violent storms; and hail. Broken branches littered my yard, and canceled plans littered my calendar.

"Where is Noah?" I asked. "Is his ark about to pass us by?" I teased my coworkers as we looked out my office window at the sheets of rain falling on the parking lot.

But what I was really looking for was a rainbow.

Don't we all hope for the rainbows? Aren't we all searching for some beauty after the pain, some encouragement after the rain?

But for the longest time, I couldn't find one.

"Look for the sun," my husband reminded me. "Both the sun and rain are needed at the same time to create a rainbow."

And then … It. Happened.

On our way to dinner, we drove through the middle of a perfect rainbow. Glorious colors — red, orange, yellow, green, blue, indigo and violet — on both sides of a giant arch with the ends close to each side of the road. Our car slowed to a saunter under the middle of a breathtakingly beautiful array of color.

My sweet sister, Liese, calls this "a kiss from God." A kiss or God-wink is an aha! moment when our loving heavenly Father provides a reminder that He is always with us and knows what we need.

This rainbow reminded me of the promises from our loving, caring Creator that joy does come after times of drought — and it does come after long nights of doubt. Most comforting to me was the realization that I didn't have to wait until the rain had ended to see a rainbow. Both sun and rain are needed at the same time.

In my soul I was reminded of God's faithfulness. It was as if He said to me: *I am here. I am here in the rain. I am here in your pain.*

Soon after I noticed God's sign in the sky, and I caught my breath, I began to sing the chorus of a poem I had written years before:

> In the midst of storms, rainbows are born,
> His love shines through our tears.
> In the midst of storms, rainbows are born,
> He is here, He is here.

He loves you, my sweet sister. He promises to be with you through the storm. Just as Noah and his family stepped off the ark to realize the beautiful bow in the sky, the fresh, arched piece of God's gift of glory covers the roads you embark on.

Sweet surprises are ahead for you.

Your part is simple. … Just like my husband encouraged me, "Look for the Son."

Hope Resurrects Our Broken Hearts

KRISTIN VANDERLIP

"Behold, the hour is coming, indeed it has come, when you will be scattered, each to his own home, and will leave me alone. Yet I am not alone, for the Father is with me. I have said these things to you, that in me you may have peace. In the world you will have tribulation. But take heart; I have overcome the world." John 16:32-33 (ESV)

I remember the morning after I stumbled upon the secret email that broke my heart. As day dawned, my tired, swollen eyes stared out the frosty window at the blanket of fog blockading any view of the sun. I sat in my empty living room, lost and alone. I cupped my hands around a ceramic mug filled with hot tea as though I were cupping the broken pieces of my heart and wept.

After losing my child and my father a few years before, I thought I'd paid my dues when it came to pain and suffering. Yet here I was again. "This can't be happening" was stuck on repeat. My rash reaction was to reject the reality of another life-altering heartache. But I knew the resistance would birth bitterness and would batter my heart into hopelessness. I returned to what I had learned in the past: gently accept the pain and aim my heart at hope.

This is what Jesus taught and modeled. In John 16:32-33, He told His disciples: *"Behold, the hour is coming, indeed it has come, when you will be scattered, each to his own home, and will leave me alone. Yet I am not alone, for the Father is with me. I have said these things to you, that in me you may have peace. In the world you will have tribulation. But take heart; I have overcome the world."*

Jesus warned that life would unfold in unexpected, painful ways. He plainly told them (and us), *"In the world you will have tribulation"* (John 16:33b). Trouble, tribulation and unexpected pain are at times unavoidable. We may want to scatter or metaphorically run in our own ways, or we can "take heart" in the heartbreak. How can we do this? These verses reveal the answer:

Though the world gives us trouble, God gives us peace. (John 16:33)
Though we may feel alone, God is with us. (Matthew 1:23; John 14:23)
Though we wait for hope to come, God bestows His hope upon us now. (Ephesians 1:14)

Hope is not found in a life void of trouble or in quick fixes to our pain. Hope resurrects our hearts as we accept the path of pain, remember God's presence and go forward in His peace. Hebrews 12:2 tells us that Jesus *"...for the joy that was set before him endured the cross..."* (ESV). Fixing our hearts on our suffering, risen Savior, and on the joy of hope set in us and before us, propels us forward through the paralysis of heartache.

My daughter and father weren't healed, yet I endured in hope. My marriage was devastated, and there was no promise of restoration, but I would endure in hope. Jesus' presence, comfort and peace meet us in the fog and tears as He cups His hands around the pieces of our hearts.

Through the most severe wounds, the darkest nights and the foggiest days, we have an unshakeable hope sustaining and strengthening us, one step at a time.

The Home for My Heavy Hope

GINA DUKE

"It is better to go to a house of mourning than to go to a house of feasting, for death is the destiny of everyone; the living should take this to heart." Ecclesiastes 7:2 (NIV)

After my mother's brain surgery was complete, I texted my pastor an update. He replied with a question: "How do people who don't know Jesus get through things like this?"

I had no idea. I couldn't imagine what people without faith in Jesus do with a heavy hope like mine because I was struggling myself.

King Solomon made an interesting observation about hard times when he said, *"It is better to go to a house of mourning than to go to a house of feasting..."* (Ecclesiastes 7:2). Really? Because I much prefer gathering for a good meal with friends versus a visit to the funeral home. So what point was he trying to make?

Solomon knew that people live toward a house of feasting. We enjoy looking forward to our next home improvement project, vacation destination and movie release, don't we?

To answer my pastor's question, this is how most people get by in life. And it is an empty pursuit because a house of feasting will always leave us needing more.

Solomon also knew that when we go to a house of mourning it un-spoils us from the running, doing and playing of life. At a funeral home, we begin to think about serious things, like eternal life and human suffering, and less about ourselves.

When my mother entered a four-year hospice stay, I was in a house of mourning long before her funeral. A house of mourning can be a quiet bout of depression, a financial blow due to job loss, or a dramatic loss of a precious friendship. It can be any season that is accompanied by grief and heartbreak.

During my mother's extended illness, my husband sensed I needed a getaway from work and worry. Once I agreed, I began to look forward to getting away anytime I was feeling downhearted. I would say to myself things like "I can't wait to get to the beach" and "Only six more weeks until I can get some relief!"

After making these sentiments my go-to for comfort, I sensed my heavenly Father's displeasure. It was clear that He did not want me to place my heavy hope toward a house of feasting that would only leave me feeling empty. So I repented.

Afterward, whenever sadness would seep in, I would place my heavy hope in Jesus. I would recall when Mary fell at the feet of Jesus to weep over the death of her brother Lazarus, and He wept with her. I would remember that Samuel, a boy who probably missed his mother, slept in the Holy of Holies, the place nearest to God. And I would hope in eternal life because Jesus said He has prepared a place for me and my mother.

In Him, my house of mourning has found a home for my heavy hope.

When God Speaks Through Cabbage

GLORIA HSU

"My sheep listen to my voice; I know them, and they follow me." John 10:27 (NIV)

I don't remember all the circumstances surrounding that day. But all I really need to remember is that I had a newborn recently diagnosed with Down syndrome, was raising four boys under the age of 8, and was too tired to go buy the cabbage needed to make the dumpling soup I was suddenly craving. I would have to let go of my simple longing for soup that day. But somehow it didn't feel simple.

The doorbell rang, and a woman I had met once was standing there smiling, holding a head of cabbage in her hands. "We were hiking when I saw a man selling cabbage, and I thought of you." Stunned, tears filled my eyes.

Do you ever feel exhausted from trying desperately to learn what God's voice sounds like? Do you find it difficult to believe it's possible that He really cares enough to show up in your seemingly little things? Do you find it easier to look for Him in your spoken prayers rather than the unspoken longings of your heart? John 10:27 had become my feeble heart's cry in those years: *"My sheep listen to my voice; I know them, and they follow me."*

There were times I had almost given up hope that I would ever understand what His voice really sounded like. It was difficult for me to comprehend and believe that He would actually speak in such detailed and caring ways specifically for me. I wouldn't have known to look for Him there, among my prayers unspoken or my longings buried deep. I had somehow missed three very important words in the middle of this beautiful verse: *"... I know them ..."*

While we are learning to recognize God's voice and follow Him, He is already fully knowing us. While I was looking for His voice in barely audible whispers or earth-quaking signs, He was showing me that His voice was right there in the gift of a cabbage, in the gift of being known. Remembering this moment, I can hear God's words underneath my friend's words: "This cabbage is from Me. See how well I know you? I delight to bring you good gifts, to comfort you in your confusion, to give you rest in your weariness and to meet you in your longings. Can you hear Me? This is My voice. I don't want you to miss Me in the small things, in your everyday. I am here, speaking now."

We can learn to know His voice because He knows us first. Isaiah 65:24 tells us, *"Before they call I will answer; while they are still speaking I will hear"* (NIV). While we are searching for Him, He is finding us. While we are waiting and longing, He is speaking and answering. Sometimes, He even comes right up to our door and rings the bell.

I Lack Nothing

RACHEL TAYLOR

"The LORD is my shepherd, I lack nothing." Psalm 23:1 (NIV)

I thumbed through the book I was reading, all the while feeling a bit motionless and numb on the inside. Then a verse jumped out at me. It was Psalm 23:1, which says, *"The LORD is my Shepherd, I lack nothing."* I paused and thought: *Then why do I feel like I am lacking so much? Lord, I have lost people I deeply love. Things look a way that I never imagined they would look. Why does life look like this? I feel so lonely.*

With that, I closed the book and went on about the day, but my thoughts continued to roll on. God was obviously highlighting something in me that I had not realized was there.

What about you? Have you asked God for things that didn't happen? Prayed prayers time and time again that didn't seem to be answered? Did things happen that knocked you flat off of your feet? Have you experienced such crushing pain and loss that you didn't know if you would even make it out alive?

I feel your pain, dear one. Yet it is in the grief-filled moments that the Lord makes Himself known to us. We can't always see the way or understand why things are going the way they are. But it is in these times that the Lord asks us to simply trust that He will indeed work for our good. It is in these difficult times that He

shines His light on the next step we are to take, and He continues to do so until we are free.

Sometimes I forget Jesus experienced rejection and grief, too. Everything I feel, He also felt. There is something comforting about that. Knowing I am not alone in my pain, even when I feel alone in it. Within 30 minutes of putting my book down, I opened the Bible app on my phone and laughed out loud. The verse of the day was Psalm 23:1, *"The LORD is my Shepherd, I lack nothing."*

I closed my eyes and said, "OK, God, I'm going to trust You in this. I'm going to trust that, even though I feel like I am lacking, that isn't true. My feelings are lying to me because You say that You are my Shepherd and I lack nothing."

Circumstances didn't automatically change, but in that moment, I knew God had me, and He would give me everything I needed. After all, He has proven Himself trustworthy in my life time and time again. So I breathed in hope. I breathed in peace. I aligned my thoughts with His thoughts, and I whispered to myself once again, but knowing it to be true this time, "I lack nothing."

How To Be Certain of Hope in Uncertain Days

LAURA ANSLOW

"Yet this I call to mind and therefore I have hope: Because of the LORD's great love we are not consumed, for his compassions never fail. They are new every morning; great is your faithfulness." Lamentations 3:21-23 (NIV)

I will never forget that day. As my husband walked through the door, the look on his face told me the meeting did not go well. His eyes were heavy, and his shoulders bore an unexpected weight. They had closed his division of the company, and he had just been made redundant. My breath caught in my throat, and my only response was an embrace.

As I lay in bed that night, my mind started racing. The questions were flowing. Fear was knocking on the door of my heart. *What now, Lord?* We had just purchased our new home four months earlier, so we had a new mortgage, four children and no job. *How will we survive this? How is this part of your plan for us, Lord?*

Uncertainty can do that. It can cause fear and doubt to attack our minds. So, right there, I stopped those thoughts before they could take hold of my heart, and I turned to His Word. I needed hope to get me through this season of uncertainty.

As I read through the prophet's words in the book of Lamentations, I could see the people of Jerusalem knew about suffering and uncertainty. Their situation may have been different from mine, but their source of hope was the same.

"Yet this I call to mind and therefore I have hope: Because of the LORD's great love we are not consumed, for his compassions never fail. They are new every morning; great is your faithfulness." (Lamentations 3:21-23)

Even though we faced uncertain days ahead, as I recalled His faithfulness, my heart filled with hope. When I remembered His great love for us, the doubts and the fear dwindled away. I began to remember God's peace as we first walked through our new home and the joy as we moved into the place He had provided for us.

I called to mind His consistent provision throughout our lives. A meal from a neighbor when I was sick, an encouraging word from a friend at just the right time. He has always been faithful to His promise to provide for our needs. (Philippians 4:19)

As I read those verses again, I realize this is the way to hope: I need to remember His faithfulness. I need to remind myself that His love is everlasting and will carry us through these hard, unknown days.

Despite the sudden changes in our lives, His goodness does not change. God does not change. The Word tells us that *"Jesus Christ is the same yesterday and today and forever"* (Hebrews 13:8, NIV). That means the God who has always provided a way through the storms of life will provide a way through this, too.

Even though we don't know what the days ahead will hold, we do know that He holds each one. We can be certain that God's great love for us will never change. We know that He is faithful to His promises. Therefore, we can be certain of our hope even in seasons of uncertainty.

Still Standing

ANGELA ANDERSON

"… stand firm thus in the Lord, my beloved." Philippians 4:1 (ESV)

It was almost like a dream come true. I gazed in awe at the dimensions standing right there in front of me: tall, dark, stately and strong. As I watched the video of my brother's trip to the Redwood Forest, I was amazed by all of those beautiful trees! Even though I was not physically in the forest, this homemade, virtual tour was breathtaking.

My favorite part of this video was the segment about the Immortal Tree. I learned that this amazing redwood stood almost 300 feet tall and 14 feet wide in diameter. The Immortal Tree had been through some of the worst experiences, yet it still remained in that forest, thriving heartily. This tree was struck by lightning, which severed the top, decreasing its height by almost 50 feet. Next, there was a fire that consumed the trees in that forest, but the Immortal Tree did not burn down. Decades later, there was a flood that washed away many of the trees, but the Immortal Tree could not be moved. And then loggers came to chop the tree down, but they gave up because the Immortal Tree was not giving way. To this day, there is a piece of an ax still stuck in the trunk of the tree, as well as scars in the tree's bark from the lightning strike, fire and flood.

Nonetheless, the Immortal Tree is still standing strong.

Many of us can identify with the Immortal Tree. The year 2020 ushered calamity and uncertainty into our lives. Perhaps tragedy struck you like lightning. You may have experienced the death of a loved one, which severed a bond, and now a piece of you is missing. Maybe you lost a job, and part of your identity was lost along with that job. Whatever the loss, at this moment you may not feel whole, but let me remind you that *you are still standing*.

Maybe fire in the form of hard times and insurmountable challenges threatened to consume you. The pandemic and quarantine placed you in isolation, and you've never felt so alone. The economic downturn came over you like a flood leaving you to drown in financial ruin. So-called friends tried to cut you down with their words instead of lifting you up with their actions. Through the fire and the flood, you may have scars, but *you are still standing*.

God's Word makes it noticeably clear that we are to stand when we are in the thrall of life. Ephesians 6:10 gives us hope that we can *"be strong in the Lord and in the power of His might"* (NKJV). We just need to stand, clothed in the whole armor of God, and He will fight for us!

In times of uncertainty, our hope lies in God and His ability to save. Yes, life may have worn us down, but by the grace of our Almighty God, we are still standing!

Confessions of a Recovering Basket Case

TINA RAIN

"I removed the burden from their shoulders; their hands were set free from the basket." Psalm 81:6 (NIV)

I was fearful of so many things. My anxiety was affecting me physically with panic attacks and gastrointestinal issues. I was stressed to my absolute limit and I could not see the light at the end of the tunnel … not this time.

During this very long and emotional season, I was ready to give up on believing in anything or anyone having the ability to be good, including me.

One afternoon, while doing housework, I had a bit of a wrestling match with God: *I'm done. I don't want to hope anymore. I can't do what You want me to do because I don't know how!*

I washed another load of laundry and felt the Holy Spirit impress something on my heart: *Put it in the basket.* Naturally, I assumed it was about laundry. The impression came a second time. When things are impressed on you that you can't explain, you know they must come from God. But even so, I ignored it.

I continued with my chores. Impending doom and uncertainties fought for space in my thoughts. Again: *Put it in the basket.* This time I stopped what I was doing, and as random tears spilled over, I questioned: *What does that even mean? Put WHAT in the basket?* Another impression: *Everything.*

When I let this sink in, a visual invaded my thinking. Jesus. Jesus standing with outstretched arms and a compassionate smile on His face. At His feet … a basket.

He beckoned me, with a slight wave of His hand, to place my worries, uncertainties, fears, anxieties, false assumptions and lost hopes into the basket. He offered to carry it away. In that moment, I realized He wants to sort through the things that concern me. If they are legitimate concerns, He will instruct me on how to proceed. But if my concerns are imaginings of my own doing, He discards them. My load lightens.

When I search the Scriptures, I see what He wants me to see: *"I removed the burden from their shoulders; their hands were set free from the basket"* (Psalm 81:6). Tears threaten as I ponder His eagerness to be exactly what I need Him to be, my basket carrier.

I might have temporarily lost hope, but I could never permanently lose hope in the One who chooses to carry what life has thrown at me.

I confess I sometimes reach for that basket of worries. When I do, I remind myself that I'm a recovering basket case and no longer need to shoulder the heavy burdens of life.

HOPE DURING

TIMES OF

UNCERTAINTY

Confident Hope Despite an Uncertain Tomorrow

JESS HALL

"... Put your hope in God, for I will yet praise him, my Savior and my God." Psalm 42:5c (NIV)

"Hope" was a word I casually used, treating it more like a wish.

"I hope it stops raining."
"I hope to go on a beach vacation."
"I hope this outfit makes me look beautiful."

I wished as I hoped, holding on to my dreams, my desires and my plans. I wished for a loving husband, a successful job, a perfect house.

I wished — anticipating for life to go my way — until an unplanned hysterectomy, divorce and job loss came true. Then I stopped anticipating and stopped hoping, falling into depression.

My perfect plans turned into an uncertain future.
Uncertain who to turn to.
Uncertain who to talk to.
Uncertain who to trust.

Then a portion of a verse whispered into my uncertainty: "... *Put your hope in God ...*" (Psalm 42:5c).

Hope? I didn't know what hope was anymore. I so desperately wanted to understand. God still had a plan to make my every wish come true ... right?

I looked up every Bible verse that had the word "hope" in it. I searched. I studied. I struggled. And then I looked up the definition.

"HOPE: to expect with confidence: TRUST" (Merriam-Webster).

This simple definition changed my perception. I reread that whispered verse with new eyes.

Put my confidence in God ...
Put my trust in God ...

We can pray to God, not wishing for our heart's desire but fully expecting with confidence that He hears us and trusting that He will help us. We can trust in who He is, the source of all hope. (Romans 15:13)

When our hope is in God, hope does not disappoint. (Romans 5:5) Hope leads to joy, (Romans 12:12) boldness, (2 Corinthians 3:12) faith and love (Colossians 1:4-5) no matter what seasons life may bring.

Only God is our refuge and strength.
Only God can heal.
Only God can protect.
Only God can provide.

My wishes for me turned into hope in Him.

And I knew, even in the midst of uncertainty, His unfailing love surrounded me, and His perfect plan for me would never change.

Yesterday had pains, and tomorrow may bring problems, but today I have peace. Today I confidently hope — I put my trust in who God is — and I sing praises to His Holy Name. "... *the LORD's unfailing love surrounds the one who trusts in him.*" (Psalm 32:10, NIV)

Finding Hope Between a Rock and a Hard Place

TINA SAVANT GIBSON

"You hem me in behind and before, and you lay your hand upon me. Such knowledge is too wonderful for me, too lofty for me to attain." Psalm 139:5-6 (NIV)

My holy tank was hovering on empty.

Christmas was approaching, but I just couldn't get into it. Not the music. Not the shopping. Not the decorating. Not even the reason for the season.

My tightly held excuses (aka: pandemic weirdness) weren't cutting it anymore. The truth was that I was craving the cutout-sugar-cookie smell of the way things used to be. Determined, with nothing but desperation, I put on my worn-out walking shoes and headed towards the wilderness trail.

That's what I called it. Actually, it was a path in a nearby park, overflowing with trees, babbling brooks and sweet solace to my pandemic-weary soul. My heart was tender as my inner Charlie Brown pleaded with arms held high, "Is there anyone who knows what Christmas is all about?"

My answer was hidden in plain sight. A tiny manger scene, vintage like me, surrounded by dried-out leaves, drizzled with dirt, nestled between two rocks. Hemmed in hope.

It reminded me of a psalm: *"You hem me in, behind and before, and you lay your hand upon me. Such knowledge is too wonderful for me, too lofty for me to attain"* (Psalm 139:5-6).

I'd almost missed the answer to my question, and I wondered, *How many others have almost missed Him, too?*

As darkness moved in, I headed home, intent on returning tomorrow to capture a photograph. The next morning, it was raining like crazy. I didn't care. I put on my tall boots, boldly faced the wind and started my walk back to those rocks. The closer I got, the faster my heart began to beat. *What if he isn't there?*

How many times have I pondered the same thing when I prayed?

But he was there, a plastic baby Jesus lying in a manger, arms wide open, covered with dirt and debris. A beautiful reminder of that silent night, holy night, over 2,000 years ago when there was no room at the inn. When heaven came to earth, unexpectedly, yet exactly on time.

What if we really believed that truth? In a global pandemic or on a random Tuesday?

When life feels like we're hiding between a rock and a hard place, there's hope.

His name is Jesus. He isn't plastic; He's perfectly alive. Just like that first Christmas, just like our next Christmas. Just like forever. Nothing is a surprise to Him, not the pandemic. No-thing. He welcomes us just the way we are, our dried-out souls covered with dirt and debris, soot and sin.

In every question, every doubt, every tear — in everything — we are hemmed in by Him. And amidst that wonderful, lofty knowledge that is beyond our human grasp, the Almighty holds us, loves us and promises we are never alone. Rest in that truth, beloved. Sleep in heavenly peace.

The Painful Pause

JEN ALLEE

"Both Mary Magdalene and the other Mary were sitting across from the tomb and watching." Matthew 27:61 (NLT)

I don't recommend job hunting during a worldwide pandemic.

We all have a woeful tale from 2020, and mine was my husband's unemployment. Initially, he was optimistic about the search, but as the job market screeched to a halt, so did his hope.

Suddenly, we faced an uncertainty that had no dead-line. We begged God to provide, trying desperately to walk by faith in the midst of a nationwide hiring freeze.

I dubbed that season the Painful Pause. Thankfully, though, we weren't the first to experience one.

The day between the crucifixion and the resurrection was a standstill for those who had pledged to follow Jesus. They had been reorienting their lives around this self-proclaimed Messiah, and now He was dead. And for them, it wasn't a pause. Death was final. This was the Painful End.

Or so they thought.

We often read this story with the end in mind, but today let's linger on day two. Not much is written about the middle day of this trilogy. We don't memorize these verses or frame them on our walls. Yet they paint an accurate picture of waiting, and they offer a message embedded for our anxious hearts.

After Jesus' body was laid to rest, the Bible states that *"Both Mary Magdalene and the other Mary were sitting across from the tomb and watching"* (Matthew 27:61).

After Jesus died, these women didn't return home, cook dinner and discuss their crazy day. They didn't shrug and walk away, thinking, *Huh, I expected Jesus to do more...*

No. They sat. They watched. They wondered. I picture them staring at the tomb while others were milling about, resuming daily activity.

Was He really the Son of God?
What about all His promises?
Can they still be trusted?

God sometimes allows life to grind to a halt because it forces our rubber faith to meet the road. When we're confronted with uncertainty, fears, doubts and insecurities pile up behind us, knocking us and our faith off balance. And like these women, we stare off into our own Painful Pauses, asking the same questions. We sit. Wondering. Watching from a distance.

Our rubber faith scraping against the road.

By "faith" I don't mean a naïve assumption that everything will be just fine. Faith is not a Pollyannaish, pat answer. Faith is knowing Jesus can be trusted despite any uncertainty trying to contradict Him.

As those dear women sat and stared at the tomb, uncertainty filled their airspace, stifling any rational thoughts that could lead to peace.

Until the next day.

The following morning, they discovered Jesus was undeniably real and powerful. Their Painful Pause was transformed into a glorious sprint!

Jesus is not a fraud nor lying in a tomb. Stand firm knowing your Painful Pause is only preparing you to experience Him anew. After nine agonizing months, my husband was gainfully employed again, and God's provision during that season was unmistakable.

So hang on, and don't get stuck on day two. A new day will dawn, shedding light on His unceasing faithfulness.

Relocate Your Hope

LESLIE JONES

"He gives strength to the weary and increases the power of the weak. Even youths grow tired and weary, and young men stumble and fall; but those who hope in the LORD will renew their strength. They will soar on wings like eagles; they will run and not grow weary, they will walk and not be faint." Isaiah 40:29-31 (NIV)

I'd run almost two hours that chilly, pre-dawn morning, the sun still below the horizon. I'll never make it, I thought, passing mile 8 in a 13.1-mile half-marathon. Weak, weary and uncertain I could continue, I slowed to a walk. With miles of struggle still to endure, my hope of crossing the finish line drained away.

"God, my strength is gone," I whimpered. "I can barely see the road and I just want to quit. Please help me." As tears threatened to spill over, I felt the Holy Spirit whisper, "I see what's ahead, so don't stop. Relocate your hope to Me, and I will renew your strength."

Oh, how it's tempting to quit when we can't see much of the road we're on. Uncertain of where we're headed, we often place hope in our own strength, believing we just need to grit our teeth and gut it out. But hope located in anything other than God will always leave us weak and weary. When we relocate our hope to the One who sees beyond the horizon, He will renew our strength to press on.

Isaiah 40: 29-31 reminds us that *"He gives strength to the weary and increases the power of the weak. Even youths grow tired and weary, and young men stumble and fall; but those who hope in the LORD will renew their strength. They will soar on wings like eagles; they will run and not grow weary, they will walk and not be faint."*

It's reassuring to know when we're weak with uncertainty, we can tap into the source of all strength and power. So how do we take our hope and relocate it to Him? Let's look at some practical ways to receive the renewed strength God promises:

- Reflect on the times God has guided you through uncertainty, and be reminded that He'll make the next step visible in His perfect timing.
- Reject the lie that you can do it on your own, and replace it with renewed commitment to rely on His strength alone.
- Relocate hope to Him, confident that, while your perspective is limited, His is unlimited.

I still couldn't see what lay ahead as I resumed my pace, yet as I placed my hope in Him, a supernatural strength propelled me forward. An hour later as the sun peeked over the desert horizon, golden rays lit up the road. I saw the finish line in the distance and knew with certainty that in His strength I would reach the end.

We overcome uncertainty when our hope is in Him to light the road before us and increase our power to keep going. As the only One who sees beyond the horizon, God promises to renew our strength when we relocate our hope to Him.

Please Stand By

LINDSEY TREW

"And the LORD God made for Adam and for his wife garments of skins and clothed them." Genesis 3:21 (ESVUK)

It was something I didn't plan for. It casually slid its way in, taking up residence. Staking claim in the deep. Uncertainty never asks permission, and at 30 that's where I found myself. Divorced, no home, no money, two small children to love … and the future that was once clear grew cloudy and hard to see. Then God came, and in the midst of the uncertainty He offered hope.

One verse, read and skimmed a hundred times, now popped off the page: *"And the LORD God made for Adam and for his wife garments of skins and clothed them"* (Genesis 3:21).

I wonder what it was like that day. I imagine a scene like no other. Heads in hands. Sitting in the cool of the afternoon. Hearts breaking, hopes fading, emptiness creeping in. Adam and Eve had made a critical error. Their future? Uncertain. And then … God did something. Read too fast and you miss it.

In the heartbreaking emptiness, God showed up. His gentle hands sewed lives back together, every seam laced with grace, every thread lined with love, every garment brushed with hope. He saw their need and filled it. Instead of leaves that would crumble and break, He gave them skins that would last. Through His compassion, He offered hope. Hope that the future could be endured.

God does the same for us. Though uncertainty creeps in, we can rest knowing that our God will see us through. He will make us new clothes to stand against the storm. And just like for Adam and Eve, He handcrafts these clothes just for us. Seams laced with grace, threads lined with love and all of it brushed with hope.

How To Hope Fully When "Hopefully" Fails

AMY LIVELY

"Therefore, preparing your minds for action, and being sober-minded, set your hope fully on the grace that will be brought to you at the revelation of Jesus Christ." 1 Peter 1:13 (ESV)

For just a few seconds, I almost forgot.

I almost forgot the pandemic that infected us with disease and death, fear and worry. I almost forgot the grieving families, courageous caregivers, exhausted essential workers, anxious unemployed and the lonely neighbor I barely took the time to notice on a good day — let alone this string of very, very bad days.

Cuddled under the covers, for just a few seconds I could almost imagine I'd open my eyes to a perfectly normal day.

I almost forgot the horrific and senseless deaths of image-bearers of God, which sparked outrage across the country as voices loudly demanded attention to racism, prejudice and discrimination.

I almost forgot the wildfires and murder hornets — in an election year, no less.

These few forgetful seconds were the best part of my day, before my sweet dreams drifted away and reality settled in like a dark cloud. Where do I go to get my "old normal" back?

These are the moments when our faith in God collides with real life, and crises pile up like cars on an icy interstate. When life as we know it is upended and interrupted, we grope through the ambiguity like a car with a burned-out headlight. We drift between the lanes of dark hopelessness and dim hopefulness. ...

It's hopeless — she'll never get better.
    Hopefully my mom will recover.
It's hopeless — this marriage is over.
    Hopefully the rumors aren't true.
It's hopeless — my prodigal child is too far gone.
    Hopefully my son will be safe.
It's hopeless — we'll never get along.
    Hopefully our nation will heal.

"Hopeless" sees no possibility of success, and "hopefully" is just an expression of my desired outcome for my current circumstances based upon my feelings. Grammatically, "hopefully" is an adverb that modifies the rest of the sentence. It's structurally dispensable: You can toss it out and lose nothing except the speaker's emotion about the real subject. "Hopefully" is an expression of how I feel about what I'm about to say. If we pry these emotional words apart, in the tiny space between them we invite God's power to enter in.

"Therefore, preparing your minds for action, and being sober-minded, set your hope fully on the grace that will be brought to you at the revelation of Jesus Christ." (1 Peter 1:13)

Oh, what a difference a space makes!

Hope encompasses all your expectations, confidence, assurance and anticipation. Peter describes it as a *"living hope"* (1 Peter 1:3b, ESV) that is active, alive, full of breath, fresh, strong, efficient, powerful and thriving. Hope isn't a wish; it's a grounded reality based on the promises of God.

Hope isn't a longing — it's a knowing.

To hope fully means your confidence, trust and reliance are perfectly, completely, entirely and steadfastly established and rooted in Jesus Christ.

Hope isn't an escape from reality — it's a real person.

Hope is not a wish for a happy ending someday.

Hope is a decision to trust God today.

When "hopefully" fails, hope fully in Jesus.

Hope for the Waiting Heart

LAUREN HILL

"Wait on the LORD; Be of good courage, And He shall strengthen your heart;
Wait, I say, on the LORD!" Psalm 27:14 (NKJV)

The light shone through the window giving the room just enough light that was comforting. The sound of my daughter's blood pressure cuff inflating every hour and the distant voices that filled the hallways were the sounds during one of the most uncertain times we have walked through as a family. Sounds that I became grateful for because they meant I still had my daughter.

I stared at the scripture that was taped to the back of my daughter's hospital crib. It was Psalm 27:14, *"Wait on the LORD; Be of good courage, And He shall strengthen your heart; Wait, I say, on the LORD!"* Her heart was failing, and she was in desperate need of a new heart.

As I looked at the word "*strengthen*," I said a prayer that God would make my daughter's half-heart whole. It was hard to have a clear picture of the future; the future that I once dreamed of for our family seemed muddled.

During every echocardiogram of her heart, I waited in anticipation, hoping the ultrasound tech would be stunned to see a whole heart on the screen. But that's not how God would heal her. No, our miracle would come in a different form.

So, while we waited, we hoped.

Friend, I am not sure what your life looks like at this moment. You may be in a season of waiting, a season of joy or a season of uncertainty. Whatever season you may find yourself in, I want to encourage you that you can have hope where you are right now. A hope that anchors your soul, hope that lasts in any season.

Hope that is in God and not our circumstances is the thread that can hold us together when our world seems to be unraveling.

Hope in a God who is steadfast, strong, immovable, loving and who can bring good from any situation.

I see the whole heart that I always prayed for now beating strong during checkups. I think of the family who said "yes" to organ donation, and I think of the hope that filled their hearts when they said "yes" to giving others a second chance at life.

That summer, not only did my daughter receive her new heart, but my heart was spiritually strengthened by the Lord. My faith was made stronger, and my courage grew more during the waiting — strength and courage that I can only attribute to a God who is so gracious to give it to me.

And, friend, He wants to give that to you, too. Maybe that is what our different seasons are about — pointing us to our one true source of strength and hope that can only be found in Jesus. A hope that enters our heart and gives us courage and strength while we wait for the storm to pass.

Ever-Changing World, Never-Changing God

MANDY JOHNSON

"May the God of hope fill you with all joy and peace in believing, so that by the power of the Holy Spirit you may abound in hope." Romans 15:13 (ESV)

Are You sure?

These three words spilled out of my mouth like a cup of water being dropped on a hardwood floor. I wanted to quickly take them back and wipe them clean, but I knew God heard me questioning Him in my prayers. *God, are You sure You're working for my good? Are You sure You're with me always? Are You sure You know what You're doing?*

Ashamed at my lack of trust, I opened my eyes and lowered my gaze, realizing how much I tend to crave answers over ambiguity, and certainty over uncertainty.

I think if we're being honest with ourselves, in the privacy of our quiet time or in the community of trusted friends, we create plans in hopes God will submit to them. We know He's God and we know He loves us, but when life feels uncertain, it feels like He should do some confessing — like He's the one who needs to reevaluate His plans.

Running low on hope and high on doubt, we can easily face uncertainty with a skewed view of just how much God loves us.

The Apostle Paul knew what it felt like to run low on hope, too. He experienced firsthand what it felt like to question Jesus and also what it felt like to place his hope in Him. Paul offers us prayerful encouragement through Romans 15:13, which says, *"May the God of hope fill you with all joy and peace in believing, so that by the power of the Holy Spirit you may abound in hope."* At the time, Paul was praying over the Christians in Rome, but his prayer can be applied to us today.

Through the power of the Holy Spirit, we can overflow with confidence, knowing God is who He says He is. He's a constant source of peace and joy, and He offers abounding hope when we trust Him. In an ever-changing world, our hope can be placed in a never-changing God.

He genuinely cares about your circumstances, questions and plans, and He wants nothing more than to lead you in and through them. God doesn't reject or punish you when you question Him. You're His cherished, loved-beyond-belief daughter; He can handle your questions. But more than answering your questions, He wants you to trust His character, love and perfect plans for you.

As you face aching seasons of uncertainty, I hope you allow Paul's prayer to be your prayer. God generously offers us inner peace when life offers us outer turmoil. Ask the God of hope to fill you with peace and joy in believing so that you may abound in hope, too.

HOPE
WHEN
RELATIONSHIPS
FALL
APART

I Want To Help Make Jesus Famous

NICOLE LANGMAN

"I want you to know, brothers, that what has happened to me has really served to advance the gospel ..."
Philippians 1:12 (ESV)

They were not the words I was ready to hear — the best ones often aren't. Over a vanilla latte, my favorite friend harnessed her courage and loved me enough to tell me the truth.

Months earlier, my husband decided he preferred a life without me. His leaving prompted a ripple effect of brokenness and confusion that threatened to swallow me whole. Some days it felt like drowning as the rejection held my head under the waves, feeding a narrative of self-defeating beliefs. Other days it felt like sharp edges in my heart. On all the days, it felt like torture.

With glistening eyes, my sweet friend looked up from her latte and quietly said, "Your story must help make Jesus famous."

Insert holy hush.

As tears rushed in, my heart knew she was right. It was time to pivot. I had stared at the pain long enough. And when we stare too long at our brokenness, we build an unhealthy bond to it. It was time to direct my energy away from the pain and onto the purpose. Onto the Person.

Rejection confirms our greatest fear: that we are unwanted. While I knew Jesus loved me, the rejection had me in a cruel tailspin of questioning. What good was I now to the Kingdom? How could I ever recover and be useful?

Scouring the Bible for examples of rejection recovery, I discovered many stories of people using the pain of rejection to point others towards Jesus.

Joseph's brothers walked away and left him to die. Trust was broken and his sense of belonging was taken, but in his wisdom, he pivoted away from the pain and towards the One who would never abandon him. In Genesis 50:20, he told his brothers, *"As for you, you meant evil against me, but God meant it for good"* (ESV). Along the way, Joseph started to collect evidence of God's hand in his life, and as he did this, the rejection story evolved into a story of victory. Joseph recognized the divine plan in his pain, and when given the opportunity, he pointed to God.

Paul was also no stranger to suffering. In Philippians 1:12, he reminds us to view our pain as purposeful. He says, *"I want you to know, brothers, that what has happened to me has really served to advance the gospel ..."* Pain offers a platform to point people to the ultimate Source of healing and comfort.

This isn't easy, but to help make Jesus famous through our suffering, we: a.) look for evidence of His hand in the story, b.) take our focus off the rejection and lock eyes with Him, and c.) notice healing in our life and give Him glory for all of it.

When we use our pain for purpose, and we point to Jesus as the only answer for healing, two incredible things happen: We find freedom from the rejection narrative that deems us unworthy, and we get to help make Jesus famous.

Replacing Ruined Moments
With a Renewed Soul

KARA O'BYRNE

"The LORD will surely comfort Zion and will look with compassion on all her ruins;
he will make her deserts like Eden, her wastelands like the garden of the LORD.
Joy and gladness will be found in her, thanksgiving and the sound of singing." Isaiah 51:3 (NIV)

How did it happen for you? Was it a text, an email or a conversation? I remember my moments well — the phone call, the insult and once even a talent show!

Moments we wish could be erased from our history but instead are painfully etched into our memory. What do we do when our soul feels the deep pangs of betrayal? I have found the only source of comfort is at the feet of my Savior: *"The LORD will surely comfort Zion and will look with compassion on all her ruins; he will make her deserts like Eden, her wastelands like the garden of the LORD. Joy and gladness will be found in her, thanksgiving and the sound of singing"* (Isaiah 51:3).

"The LORD will surely comfort ..." No matter how deep the cut of betrayal, we can rely on our comforting Lord to show up. He promises us this, and unlike our human companions, His promises do not fail. No one can soothe our blistered souls more than His loving presence.

"... will look with compassion on all her ruins ..." Ruins are an inevitable part of our broken relationships. Some ruins are known in an instant while others play out in an unfolding drama that painfully crumbles bit by bit. Jesus looks at every piece with all-knowing compassion and understanding. The "com-" in compassion reminds us He is with us. He is passionately sitting with us in our hurt and empathizing with it.

"... he will make her deserts like Eden ..." As you sit in your splintered wreckage, the perfection of Eden seems like a far-fetched dream. When your soul stings from the slap of betrayal, to hear that God uses things for your good can almost feel cruel. But trust me, friend, I have sat where you sit, and I know He will do just as He promises. God is the author and master of renewal. We can trust that even if we are wandering in a desert wasteland, we will not stay there. He will eventually usher us into the promised land. This is only the start of His great redemption story for you.

"Joy and gladness will be found ..." Sometimes it can be hard to believe you will laugh again. When tears have been your food, and your body holds a suffocating weight, "gladness" and "thanksgiving" are not words that come to mind. Yet our King knows what we do not. He knows that with His help and perseverance, His great work can be finished in us. (James 1:2-4) There is no greater joy than when He brings us from ruined to rebuilt. You cannot help but erupt with praise and worship as you witness this unbelievable miracle.

I don't know what kind of pain has filled your world, but I do know a Savior who is worthy. He is worthy to hold our hurt and transform it into healing. Come, sit with Him and see. I promise you will not be disappointed.

Holy Hide–and–Seek With Jesus

KELLY KIRBY WORLEY

"'What I tell you now in the darkness, shout abroad when daybreak comes. What I whisper in your ear, shout from the housetops for all to hear!' Matthew 10:27 (NLT)

True to my sanguine temperament, I'm usually the most bubbly, happy person in a room, someone others look to for encouragement. But that woman suddenly deserted me when a stranger named Despair showed up at my door almost five years ago.

Despite my deep-rooted faith in Jesus, unexpected betrayal crushed my spirit, wrecked my soul and left me with a crippling case of self-doubt. What hurt most was knowing God was in control, and He was allowing my painful circumstances. I'd already given all I had to be all-in with Him, including my job and the financial security it offered. What else could He want?

My only hope was to cling to my Bible and hunker down with Jesus while praying for a miracle. It was in that dark place that I learned the meaning of Matthew 10:27, in which Jesus says, *"What I tell you now in the darkness, shout abroad when daybreak comes. What I whisper in your ear, shout from the housetops for all to hear!"*

Friends, there's miraculous power available to us when we resist the urge to stew over what's been done to us, and we lean into Jesus instead. It's in this place of ruthless trust and utter dependence God most often reveals and heals hidden wounds we've stuffed so deep we aren't aware they exist. Until those false beliefs are brought to the surface and dispelled with God's Truth, they'll keep us from living in the freedom that is ours in Christ. Had God not allowed the consequences of another's poor choices to play out in my life, I'd still be captive to a massive false belief that's been sabotaging my life since elementary school.

You see, I grew up in a single-parent home when divorce was socially unacceptable, and I remember how differently people treated us. Since this was never openly discussed, my immature brain formed its own explanation: Acceptance, security and value in life are defined by the status "wife."

Though I fervently prayed for a different outcome, letting go of what "should have been" renewed my hope and confidence in the Lord's plans for me. What He revealed to me, the way He loved me to a place of wholeness I've never known before, could not have occurred any other way. I'm convinced God reserves a special place in His heart for those of us who suffer extreme grief and despair caused by the actions of another.

When we stop defining ourselves by our failures and learn to trust and entirely rely on God's love for us, our hearts begin to open to the breathtaking discovery of the wonder of Jesus. As His ambassadors and recipients of His marvelous grace, it's our job to help others along the way.

Hope for the Future Flights of Freedom

HEATHER HUGGINS

*"The LORD will fulfill his purpose for me. LORD, your faithful love endures forever;
do not abandon the work of your hands." Psalm 138:8 (CSB)*

I push through the glass doors to enter the butterfly exhibit. The space is enormous. The natural light seeps in uninhibited thanks to walls and a ceiling made of glass. Hundreds of brilliant, colorful butterflies glide in and out of the lush plants and flowering vegetation that fill the elaborate habitat. I gaze at the flurry of their flying freedom, enjoying their beauty and grace. I am amazed at the glory of them.

I find a bench and watch as the butterflies land, drink and then fly off. As one sits and drinks, I look at the detail of this beautiful creature. I think of the journey that was required to get it to this point of perfection and purpose. That beauty came at a heavy price. I think of all that must have been required of it during its transformation in the caterpillar and chrysalis (cocoon) phases. I can relate more to this butterfly's earlier phases of crawling and constriction than its current phase of flight and glory.

After my husband left me and we divorced, I became a struggling single mom. I felt the bindings of my new cocoon. It was tight around me. My emotions were chaotic. It was dark in there. I wasn't sure what was happening or what to expect next. All I knew was that I felt trapped and scared. I crawled into prayer and into the Scriptures in a desperate search for guidance and help in this new, binding place.

In an answer to my plea, God let me hear His voice in Psalm 138:8 — *"The LORD will fulfill his purpose for me. LORD, your faithful love endures forever; do not abandon the work of your hands."*

From this scripture, I gleaned the following guidance: God's faithful love endures forever. His love and faithfulness do not run out like my husband's did. There is no limit or change; He is everlasting and can be trusted, especially in times when I am feeling bound by my difficult reality.

God will fulfill His purpose for me. From inside my chrysalis, I could not see out, but God was certainly busy at this time. He was working and changing me. Knowing that He has taken the parts of every caterpillar and rearranged them into a beautiful butterfly, I, too, can expect to be transformed into my glorious purpose.

God will not abandon the work of His hands. God is committed to His work, and we, His children, are His work. My job is to surrender and to choose to trust Him. There will be a time when I will be flying in the freedom of His handiwork, just like my butterfly friends.

From Flat to Filled

SUSAN ZURCHER

"May the God of hope fill you with all joy and peace as you trust in him, so that you may overflow with hope by the power of the Holy Spirit." Romans 15:13 (NIV)

Cardboard. Dry. Flat. That's how I would have described my marriage that day. Once again, I found myself alone. It had become my way of life, feeling like a married single woman. I wasn't sure if that was actually a thing, but I sure felt like it. My husband was missing again. The reason why, I don't remember, but there I sat alone in my car with the window open as the warm, late-afternoon sun set over the soccer field where one of my kids finished practice.

Is this what it has come to? Is this what I have to look forward to for the rest of my life?

After several years of marriage, three kids, workaholism, financial struggles and various health issues, our marriage felt dull, empty and lifeless. As if we were simply going through the motions of survival. No life, no joy, just one duty, one chore, after another. One day rolled into the next and I thanked God every night He brought me through another day.

It was around this time I learned to pray and speak God's Word. Not a "fake it till you make it" or "name it and claim it" theology but actually acting like I believed what I said I believed about God and speaking His Word over my life. I learned our warfare is *"not against flesh and blood"* but against the evil powers of the spirit world (Ephesians 6:12, NIV). Speaking God's Word not only has power in the physical world but in the spiritual as well.

I started to pray and speak God's Word out loud over my husband, marriage and children on a daily, and sometimes moment-by-moment, basis. At first my children looked at me funny, but then they just got used to their mom walking around praying Scripture out loud. While my circumstances didn't improve overnight, I could once again feel joy growing inside me day by day. God's Word was not only going out of my mouth but down into my heart. I had a renewed sense of hope for the future. It was during this time I discovered one of my favorite Scripture verses.

"May the God of hope fill you with all joy and peace as you trust in him, so that you may overflow with hope by the power of the Holy Spirit." (Romans 15:13)

That's what we get when we trust God with our lives and relationships — hope, joy and peace. He has all the power, and when we do our part, He takes care of the rest.

That was many years ago, and while my marriage will never be perfect this side of heaven, it has much improved and continues to do so. It has taken a lot of time, biblical counseling, marriage books and more, but like our relationship with the Lord, it is well worth the effort.

Glorious Transformation

CHRISTY WILLIAMS

"And we all, with unveiled face, beholding the glory of the Lord, are being transformed into the same image from one degree of glory to another." 2 Corinthians 3:18a (ESV)

I tossed the phone across my bed and buried my face in a pillow to release a much-needed scream. As the heat began to leave my body, I reread the irritating text from my dad. Why had I yet again reacted to him with annoyance instead of responding with grace? Until recently, our relationship had actually been growing since he'd been sober and consistent with his medications for a mental illness. I thought I was prepared for another relapse, but my reaction to it proved otherwise. I was so over it.

And I was mostly disappointed in myself. Instead of maturity and growth, all I could see were battle scars from 20 years of setbacks. I knew I couldn't change my dad, but changing myself and my expectations of the relationship sometimes felt impossible, like I was constantly starting over. I felt hopeless.

I happened to be refinishing an old dresser at the time. I'd taken a break from working on it because I had discovered I'd been making several mistakes sanding the wood and would have to basically start over. As I ran my hand over the raw and unfinished places in the wood, I realized all those mistakes and learned skills served as a perfect picture of the challenging relationship with my dad.

God reminded me that, just as I kept returning to refinish the dresser, He was constantly working to conform me into His image, as promised in 2 Corinthians 3:18a. The Apostle Paul wrote that those in Christ, those with *"... unveiled face, beholding the glory of the Lord, are being transformed into the same image from one degree of glory to another."* He didn't write that we are transformed in an instant into the image of Christ. Rather, we undergo transformation gradually as we become more and more like Him.

Just as a woodworker returns to a piece of furniture, gradually moving up in degrees of sanding and taking care to polish out scuffs, the Holy Spirit continually brings us back to the same challenges in difficult relationships to refine us. For me, He has been transforming my judgmental thinking, unforgiving spirit and hot-tempered anger. While we can lament the learning process, we shouldn't ignore the fact that God is always working.

We aren't starting over. We're returning to our problems with new skills and tools acquired over years through the work of the Holy Spirit.

I'm still working out things with my dad, but the dresser is finished. Every day, the beauty of the dark, stained wood reminds me of the work that the Spirit has already done in my heart to transform me. And those blemishes that I couldn't quite erase will always tell the story of the here-but-not-yet reality that I am likewise imperfect and will not be finished until I meet Christ face to face. In the meantime, the Holy Spirit has more transforming work to complete in us all. Let's joyfully join Him in the process.

HOPE

WHEN

FACING A

HEALTH

CRISIS

To Hold Our Broken–Open Hearts

"I remain confident of this: I will see the goodness of the LORD in the land of the living." Psalm 27:13 (NIV)

My living room: a spinning funhouse. Walls rocked like sides of a ship, sharp, and I was unable to focus and still the swirl.

The speech. Slow, slurred. My brain knew what it wanted to say, but words wouldn't come, anchored to another dimension I wasn't meant to reach. I am glad I was sitting on the chair at my table, or I would have found myself buckled on the floor as the world lurched and I could not catch up.

A stroke, doctors told me hours later as I lay angled in a hospital bed. At age 33. The evidence was undeniable: three white dots sparked across my cerebellum on the CT scan results.

The next few days fused, full of tests and conversations, prayers and visits from family and friends. When I could go home, I took more answers with me. A hole in my aorta caused a small blood clot to slip through the chambers of my heart and into my head. I would need a procedure to close the hole a few months later.

Life's surprises sure can slap us in our souls and try and shake the faith right out of us. How do we anchor to hope when our world jolts upside down and we are faced with unexpected news with no guarantee of a smooth journey ahead? By clinging to God's Word and taking hold of His promises.

"I remain confident of this:
I will see the goodness of the LORD
In the land of the living."
(Psalm 27:13)

When we come to a point where God guides us to experience Himself in entirely new ways, it often begins with a battle of hope. Will we dare to believe God's at work on our behalf? Hope is the healing our souls desperately crave, and the enemy will stop at nothing to twist us with lies that God will not come through.

But we dig in our heels and hold on to our Healer. He assures us of His goodness and a lasting hope found in Him. God, in His infinite care and wisdom, invites us to hold up our broken-open hearts to Him and to see that He really does have our best in mind, even when it looks different than what we imagine. We make the choice to hope and be confident in God's promises that He will fulfill His plans for our good and His glory. (Romans 8:28)

As I recovered, I rested in these promises. God is our Refuge and Good Shepherd, and He wants us to take comfort in His care. Then, our hearts aligned with Jesus, we're hope-filled with His presence and mercy.

Your Word Equips

JESSIKA SANDERS

"So the LORD said to him, 'What is that in your hand?' He [Moses] said, 'A rod.'" Exodus 4:2 (NKJV)
"But lift up your rod, and stretch out your hand over the sea and divide it." Exodus 14:16a (NKJV)

As I stood behind the sea of doctors feverishly working to stabilize my newborn son, my eyes met my husband's and silently screamed, "How are we going to make it through this?"

Although my flesh cowered at the sight of it all, deep within me, my spirit was poised and ready. You see, God has a history of equipping His children with the tools they need to endure the storms of this life.

In His holy encounter with Moses in Exodus 4:2, God showed Moses he was already equipped: *"So the LORD said to him, 'What is that in your hand?' He [Moses] said, 'A rod.'"* Chapters later, in Exodus 14:16a, when Moses and the Israelites stood before the Red Sea with Pharaoh in hot pursuit, God directed Moses to *"... lift up your rod, and stretch out your hand over the sea and divide it."* Moses' response of faith and obedience allowed room for God to part the seas, making a way through what seemed impossible.

For me, there wasn't a burning bush but rather a sacred moment on a sofa one month earlier. The Lord spoke specific instructions for the tools I held in my hands: *Read through the entire book of Psalms. Circle the parts I tell you. Pray these verses over yourself and your unborn son continuously until I tell you to stop.*

As odd as the instructions may have seemed, I trusted. I didn't know what lay ahead, but God did. Reading through the psalms, obediently underlining verses and circling stanzas, I felt like Joshua marching around the walls of Jericho. He with priests and trumpets, and I with pen and highlighter. I remained fervent in prayer as my due date approached — trusting God and boldly marching prayer circles around invisible walls until He called them to fall.

The walls didn't fall right away. We spent four excruciating weeks in the NICU. I knew I was incapable of enduring such trying circumstances in my own strength, but each circled prayer emboldened and equipped me with the hope I needed to continue praying through the storm.

Maybe you're experiencing a health crisis of your own. Maybe you're drowning in a sea of uncertainty and ever-changing circumstances. Maybe you're clinging to a piece of wreckage in the waters, or maybe you're being battered by the waves. Wherever you find yourself, I pray you find comfort in knowing you aren't expected to do this in your own strength. God has equipped you with His Word, which is everything you need to endure the storm. So open your Bible, close your eyes and allow Him to equip you with the passages that will help you through.

Jesus Goes With Us, Even to Furniture Stores

SUSAN DAVIDSON

"Have I not commanded you? Be strong and courageous. Do not be frightened, and do not be dismayed, for the LORD your God is with you wherever you go." Joshua 1:9 (ESV)

I tried to convince myself that I could do this. It was just a raggedy, old couch and chair. Easy to replace. Right?

I should have been excited to decorate my living room with the new farmhouse look I had been wanting. Instead, I found myself struggling with letting go of the old and embracing the new.

The unsightly hole in my chair wasn't the only thing exposed. It had also become more than just a trip to a furniture store. It was about one more decision I would now be solely responsible for. Yet one more thing I would now do alone because my husband's diagnosis of Multiple Sclerosis had stolen something else.

The truth was, I longed for the old. Old meant he was well. Old was comfortable and familiar. New was hard and left me feeling sorrowful and empty.

I allowed heavy tears to flow before leaving for the furniture store. I opened my Bible and pored over the passage of Scripture about the children of Israel who took 30 days to mourn the life of Moses. They took time to mourn before leaving the wilderness to embrace their new life in Canaan. (Deuteronomy 34:8-9) They should have been excited and eager to leave for this brand-new land they had dreamed of for so long. Sadly, grieving what was familiar has a way of stealing the excitement and joy from a new experience, replacing newness with sadness and dread.

This stirring message from the Israelites' journey gave me a new perspective. It comforted my grieving heart to know someone else knew how I felt. I followed their example and gave myself permission to let go of my old and familiar. I took time to grieve before moving forward to embrace the new.

As I stood to leave for the furniture store, I was reminded of another verse that reads, *"Have I not commanded you? Be strong and courageous. Do not be frightened, and do not be dismayed, for the LORD your God is with you wherever you go"* (Joshua 1:9). As I allowed that verse to soak down deep into my heart, my grieving spirit began to give way to hope. I felt a peace settle over me that I didn't think was possible.

My new normal meant my husband could no longer go with me, but something very familiar would always remain. Through every new decision I have to make, every new thing I have to learn to do all by myself, and in every situation where I find myself letting go again, Jesus is there with me. Always.

No matter what hard thing any of us are facing today, tomorrow or next week, let this be a reminder that we never go through it alone. We will find that He goes with us to the ends of the world and to all the everyday places in between — even to furniture stores.

Where Does My Hope Come From?

CARRIE HAMMONS

"May the God of hope fill you with all joy and peace in believing, so that by the power of the Holy Spirit you may abound in hope." Romans 15:13 (ESV)

My daughter was 15 months old when she began to fall off her growth curve, and we questioned for the first time if there was something wrong with her little body. By 18 months, we were in full-blown panic mode after a July Fourth weekend left us coming home from the pediatrician's office with more questions than answers.

What we knew: Her body was not working properly, and if we didn't get it straightened out fast, she was going to be very sick. What we *didn't* know: everything else. We had no idea what was causing her to be so sick or how to get her any relief. Also, what we thankfully didn't know was how long it would take to get those answers.

With every single test, I would pray, "Lord, let this be it. Please give us answers so that we can move forward in healing. Amen." Until the tests got scary, and then I would pray, "But not this one, Lord. That's too much!"

As we searched for answers from medical professionals, I searched for answers from the Lord. Most of the questions came in my darkest, weakest moments, but they gave birth to new life — my new life. I never got the specific answers I wanted; instead, my questions drew me into a deeper relationship with God, where He showed me His kindness, mercy, goodness, compassion, strength and love.

Over time, God opened my eyes to what I should have been praying for all along, and what I continue to pray to this day as we still fight for our little girl, and now her baby brother: "Lord, I pray for whatever brings You the most glory. Amen."

As I shifted my prayers away from what would bring me earthly satisfaction and momentary relief, God began to show me how I had misplaced my hope. When you spend years of your life fighting for answers while living the nightmare of a medical crisis, you begin to put your hope in one thing: a diagnosis. But God was so tender and gracious with me as He lovingly showed me where I should always place my hope — and that is in God alone.

Romans 15:13 tells us that *"… the God of hope [will] fill [us] with all joy and peace in believing, so that by the power of the Holy Spirit [we] may abound in hope."* God's Word doesn't tell us that this will happen only on the good days but that it will happen every day.

Because of our relationship with Jesus Christ, we have the Holy Spirit in us, and He fills us with His hope, His joy and His peace as we face all of life's circumstances, including the unknowns of a health crisis.

Hope Flips Our Focus From "Why" to "Who"

PAM NICHOLSON

"yet I will rejoice in the LORD; I will take joy in the God of my salvation." Habakkuk 3:18 (ESV)

Why, God? Why does my son have to suffer so much physically and emotionally at such a young age? From the time my son had emergency intestinal surgery at age 8, several surgeries at age 14 and continual pain from ages 14 to 17, I continually begged God for healing and answers. God was silent. What was I doing wrong? Was our problem a wrong doctor, a wrong diagnosis, too little faith or not enough prayer?

Many of us find ourselves at this same spiritual crossroad when we've experienced illness or pain; our prayers focus on "why." God's Word tells us about many individuals who questioned God, including Abraham, David, Isaiah, Jeremiah, Habakkuk and many others.

They chose to wait on God and to hope in His character. As they placed their hope in God, they flipped their focus from asking "why?" to asking "who?" The focus on God's faithfulness changed their perspective from despair to hope.

Habakkuk 3 gives us Habakkuk's response to God's vision for taking the Israelites through captivity and back to their land. (Habakkuk 1-2) Habakkuk responds to God by recognizing His sovereignty and faithfulness to His people. Focusing on the character of God changed Habakkuk's perspective from the immediate circumstances to the eternal faithfulness of God. Hope grew in his heart as he saw God as greater than his circumstances. By verse 18, the flip from "why" to "who" refocused Habakkuk on God's salvation.

Don't we all need hope when our circumstances seem hopeless? A few years after my son's last surgery, God broke through my questions and answered me with His faithfulness. As I drove to work and begged God to heal my son, God spoke to me. He opened my eyes to see the beautiful sunrise. I discovered a new sense of hope as I focused on His faithfulness. In that quiet moment, I realized that my faith and perspective did a flip from "why" to "who."

Through tears, I asked for forgiveness and asked God to show me more of His character, His sovereignty and His faithfulness.

This prayer and desire to know God led to a choice to grow in the knowledge of God and His Word. My hope grew, and I began to see God as greater than my circumstances. No, my son didn't experience a miracle of complete healing. However, I can look back and see how God worked through doctors, medications, teachers, family and friends to improve his health. As my focus changed to "who," my perspective shifted from despair to hope. With Habakkuk, I continue to say:

"yet I will rejoice in the LORD; I will take joy in the God of my salvation" (Habakkuk 3:18).

Misplaced Hope

KASIE SECREST

"And not only this, but we also exult in our tribulations, knowing that tribulation brings about perseverance; and perseverance, proven character; and proven character, hope; and this hope does not disappoint, because the love of God has been poured out within our hearts through the Holy Spirit ..." Romans 5:3-5 (NASB 1995)

Sometimes the hurt is too heavy, the grief is too deep, the fear is blinding and the platitudes of faith are not enough to satisfy. But thankfully, God meets us right where we are and has the remedy for our wounded souls.

He is the Balm of Gilead. When my tiny 4-year-old lay immobilized on life support for 14 days, I spoke like the psalmist to my soul: *"Put your hope in God ..."* (Psalm 42:11, NIV). My soul responded with, "Yes, but how? What if she dies? And what if she lives?" It's in this place, when we come to the realization that we have no control, that we find the true hope of God.

It's easy, in a medical crisis, to find ourselves professing hope in God when we are in fact placing our hope somewhere else entirely. We are grasping at more knowledge, more information, another procedure, a better test result, the skill of a particular doctor, or the resources or reputation of a particular hospital. Even if we profess our hope is in God, it is often misplaced. Hope placed merely in what God can do is also misplaced hope.

Many times over the course of my daughter's illness, I found myself meditating on Romans 5:3-5 and asking myself: *What is THIS HOPE that does not disappoint? What if it is not God's plan to heal my sweet girl on this side of heaven? Would I still trust Him? Would I still love Him, follow Him and praise Him?*

The kind of hope that does not disappoint is the kind that is placed in the character of God, in WHO He is, not what He can or will do. It is an open-handed hope that sits in surrender and trust. This hope does not come naturally or quickly but is a result of persevering by faith through the fire of suffering.

Scripture declares over and over that He is good. He is light, and there is no darkness in Him. (1 John 1:5) Second, He is for us and is always working for our good. (Romans 8:28) Finally, He is faithful. Paul reminds us that even if we disown God, He will never be unfaithful to us because He cannot disown Himself. (2 Timothy 2:13) Hope in this: God will never disappoint. He cannot fail.

Today we have the hope that our daughter's suffering is over, and she is fully healed in the presence of Christ. We have hope, despite our loss, because God poured His love into our hearts by the Holy Spirit. That love enabled us to carry on for our own good and His glory, and it carries us still today.

You Don't Have To Be Lonely

KRISTIN MILNER

*"And when they could not get near him because of the crowd, they removed the roof above him,
and when they had made an opening, they let down the bed on which the paralytic lay.
And when Jesus saw their faith, he said to the paralytic, 'Son, your sins are forgiven.'"* Mark 2:4-5 (ESV)

I suddenly felt forced into a club I never wanted to join. A club that requires wheelchair access for many of its members. *How can I possibly have Multiple Sclerosis? How will I raise our three daughters? Will life ever be OK again?* These were just a few of the thoughts constantly racing through my mind. I didn't know how to feel anything other than hopelessness.

In the midst of crisis, we often visualize what we are losing. The memories are close enough to long for yet too distant to reach. How can we move on when we don't want to? Sometimes we need others to carry us through these difficult moments.

In the midst of life's storms, we must surround ourselves with friends who will fight for us, doing whatever it takes to bring the hope found only in Jesus. After my diagnosis, friends and family filled our life and home with constant care. This included (but wasn't limited to) learning to distribute medications through an IV at my kitchen table while also playing with our young daughters. My loved ones' endless support helped us through very hard days.

Their greatest gift, however, was continually carrying me to see Jesus. It often felt too hard to go alone. We see this in Scripture when four friends carried a paralytic to see Jesus. This was no easy task. Jesus had returned to His hometown after performing many miracles. Large crowds awaited to see Him, but the doors to enter were too crowded to get in.

These four men knew their friend needed help only Jesus could provide. Instead of accepting defeat, they got creative and persistent. Mark 2:4-5 continues the story: *"And when they could not get near him because of the crowd, they removed the roof above him, and when they had made an opening, they let down the bed on which the paralytic lay. And when Jesus saw their faith, he said to the paralytic, 'Son, your sins are forgiven.'"*

This paralyzed man was healed because of his friends' faith!

Too often, we refuse help from others. We don't want to be an inconvenience. We try managing things alone. Alone. The good news is, our friends want to help. The hard news is, we must let them. Let them make the meals and watch the kids. Let them come sit in our living room and fold our laundry. Let them laugh with us. Then let them pray for us.

Find the friends in your life who will gladly lift you onto a roof, only to lower you back down. Cherish these friends. Let them know you are thankful for them. And when necessary, let them do whatever it takes to carry you to Jesus.

HOPE FOR THE WORN-OUT MOM

Hope for the Spilled-Cereal Mornings

JANIE PORTER

"As for me, since I am poor and needy, let the Lord keep me in his thoughts. You are my helper and my savior. O my God, do not delay." Psalm 40:17 (NLT)

A yelp over the Spiderman Lego, and a full bowl of Cheerios slams to the floor. The milk backsplash wets my forehead. My eyes darken and I can feel the fire rising in my chest.

It is only 7:48 a.m. and I am already done with this day.

I close my eyes at the kitchen sink and breathe out long and hard. The children's racket fades into the background. Another day.

Another day of the same arguments, the same messes, the same frustrations. The same things I dealt with yesterday. The same things are ahead today.

The circular tasks are unending. The work is never done. Laundry is folded as dirty clothes blanket the floor. I started the dishwasher after snack time, and now I'm starting dinner. The messes happen in the background as I start to mop up the spilled milk. It will continue all day.

Oh Lord, how I need You right now, I silently cry out from the depths of my exhausted, weary soul.

I am depleted.

I am drained.

I am shutting down.

Lord, please. I need You right now.

And I don't just need Your strength to get up early with toddlers and mop this messy floor and fold clothes.

I need Your peace. I need to know that I'm meant to be here. That I belong here.

God, remind me that You have placed me here for this divine and invisible work. That will give me the hope I need to go on.

I found an off-the-beaten-path verse today that really spoke to me. It's Psalm 40:17, which says, *"As for me, since I am poor and needy, let the Lord keep me in his thoughts. You are my helper and my savior. O my God, do not delay."*

Something about the last line really caught me.

"... O my God, do not delay."

There's an urgency in David's tone; the need is immediate. He desires the comfort only his Holy Father can provide. He is begging for God's help.

"... O my God, do not delay."

Going to the Lord with our every need is a daily practice. In this psalm, we witness David laying the groundwork for a life that is characterized by an unfailing trust in the Lord. We can join him and walk in the faith that God will do what He says He's going to do.

For some, trusting and believing that God will handle it all is a natural habit. For others, it requires a daily discipline of prayer, patience and persistence to hand over to Him all our cares, burdens and spilled-cereal mornings.

God knows what He's doing. He has it all under control. Our hope can rest in knowing that the God of the universe totally has it covered. And when we need to, we can cry out to Him.

Oh Lord, please meet me where I am today. Meet me right here in this kitchen. I need you today. Oh my God, do not delay.

When You've Tried Everything

SUSAN DAUGHERTY

"Simon answered, 'Master, we've worked hard all night and haven't caught anything. But because you say so, I will let down the nets.'" Luke 5:5 (NIV)

I took a deep breath and got in the car to go shoe shopping with my teenager. If this errand played out like usual, he wouldn't speak a word and would meet my attempts at conversation with a shrug or a grunt.

I was exhausted from the strain as my relationship with my youngest child unraveled. My grasp on hope was slipping with each new conflict over schoolwork, curfew, technology and attitude.

Teenage rebellion isn't the only time we confront discouragement as parents. It stalks us through toddler tantrums, chore wars and middle school peer drama, too. I think every parent has confronted the fear that "this isn't working" at least once as we have sought to solve a behavior or attitude issue.

We may try to work the problem harder or look for help from experts. In my case, I amassed a small library of parenting books and subscribed to podcasts. I sought advice from experienced parents and more than one counselor, each time hoping I would discover the secret formula that would turn things around.

Recently, God reminded me that my parenting style was a lot like Peter's fishing strategy, as revealed in a conversation with Jesus. After Peter loaned Jesus his boat to teach a crowd at the lakeside, Jesus told him to go fishing. Peter had already worked long and hard with no result, and he wasn't shy about making it known.

"... 'Master, we've worked hard all night and haven't caught anything. But because you say so, I will let down the nets.'" (Luke 5:5)

In other words, Peter had already tried the "right" way and time to fish, and it hadn't worked. He saw no hope of catching fish that day but grudgingly agreed to try again because he respected Jesus.

My parallel to Peter's honest response goes something like this: "Lord, I have worked night and day, and my son hasn't 'caught' anything I want to teach him or acknowledged the ways I help him. But for You, I'll try again."

In faith, we can show up for our kids one more day as we strive to love with both boundaries and grace. And just as Peter's fishing success didn't depend on the conditions that day or on his skill, a breakthrough with our children does not rest totally on our shoulders. Our hope comes from cooperating with Jesus' instructions, trusting His power is at work. We aren't supposed to quit trying, but we can give up trying to force our children to change.

As you wait and hope, dear friend, may you listen for the Spirit's guidance in the method and timing of your efforts. Stay alert to His whisper to let down your nets, and prepare to receive what He has been preparing in your children's hearts all along.

What's Hiding Your Hope?

MARY FOLKERTS

"For you have been my hope, Sovereign LORD, my confidence since my youth." Psalm 71:5 (NIV)

I was baffled when, shortly after our youngest daughter's first birthday, friends asked my husband for coffee without inviting me. That evening, he informed me I had been the primary topic of conversation. They'd expressed concern for my mental health and suggested I see a doctor. I felt like a specimen in a petri dish, sliced, splayed and examined.

Reluctantly, I made an appointment. The doctor confirmed their suspicions and prescribed antidepressants. I soon realized our friends were not judging me but had recognized signs of depression and were willing to endure my short-term wrath so that I could get help.

That was 16 years and many life lessons ago. There were seasons where I dipped low into darkness, grasping for any shred of hope and light. The demands of raising our growing family, along with the additional needs of our daughter born with Down syndrome, were sometimes too much for me to handle. How could I be a good mamma when I couldn't take care of myself? With tears streaming down my face, I would beg God for a sliver of the hope I had once known.

In Psalm 71:5, David recalls what we often forget: *"For you have been my hope, Sovereign LORD, my confidence since my youth."* Life can have a way of causing our confidence and hope in Christ to be hidden in a fog. For example, let's picture that God's steadfast hope is a massive boulder in the landscape, dependable and unmoving. But then, one day, a curtain of fog descends, shrouding the boulder of hope. The fog consists of my thoughts and fickle feelings that produce turmoil, causing lies to seem like truth. Relying on shifting emotions is a shaky foundation on which to base my beliefs.

Many life factors negatively drive our emotions, be they circumstances, personal conflicts, fatigue, burnout or depression. The enemy of our soul doesn't care what the cause is; he will use it to make us believe our hope is gone. A loss of hope is the gut-wrenching feeling of despair.

Like the psalmist, I need to revisit Truth to override my feelings of doubt. God's faithfulness in the past reminds me He is still trustworthy today. My feelings do not determine Truth, but they can cloud it. Therefore, I must keep a tight rein on my thoughts, focusing instead on God's Truth. When I am wielding His Truth, He helps me cut through the fog of lies to discover that His hope is still there.

Dear friend, it's difficult for us as moms to encourage our children in the hope of Christ when we lose sight of the hope we once clung to. In my situation, I needed professional help and good counsel to sift through and find clarity of thought. Let me encourage you that our feelings of hopelessness can never cancel the certainty of the hope Christ provides.

The psalmist reminds us of this truth: *"Why, my soul, are you downcast? Why so disturbed within me? Put your hope in God, for I will yet praise him, my Savior and my God"* (Psalm 42:11, NIV).

Always Just Beyond My Grasp

AMY MORGAN

"Are you tired? Worn out? Burned out on religion? Come to me. Get away with me and you'll recover your life. I'll show you how to take a real rest. Walk with me and work with me—watch how I do it. Learn the unforced rhythms of grace. I won't lay anything heavy or ill-fitting on you. Keep company with me and you'll learn to live freely and lightly." Matthew 11:28-30 (MSG)

Night after night, as I shuffled off to bed, discouraged from yet another day of missing the mark, my final stop was my children's bedsides. As I kissed their sweet, sleeping foreheads, I prayed, *Lord, help them love You more than I can.*

With tear-stained, desperate prayers, I pleaded that my children's faith would be stronger than mine. That delight in the Lord wouldn't be so difficult for them. That following Christ would come naturally to the next generation because for some reason that blessing felt withheld from me, always just beyond my grasp.

Like Jacob wrestling with God, I was determined to fight for this blessing, to plead my case and change their future.

One night, on my knees again, as I offered up the same plea, I felt God whisper back:

"I love YOU more than you can comprehend.
I want YOU to love Me more than you think you can.
Spend time with Me."

I was caught off guard. Instantaneously the focus shifted as the future became present.

The Father who *"...knows what you need before you ask him"* (Matthew 6:8, ESV) in His omnipotent love heard the doubt and desperation hidden in my prayer: *If I can't find joy and delight in You, Lord, I'm not sure You love me.*

Then, in His gracious love for me, *His child,* He reached out His hand beckoning me to new life, reassuring my weary soul through Jesus' invitation:

"Are you tired? Worn out? Burned out on religion? Come to me. Get away with me and you'll recover your life. I'll show you how to take a real rest. Walk with me and work with me—watch how I do it. Learn the unforced rhythms of grace. I won't lay anything heavy or ill-fitting on you. Keep company with me and you'll learn to live freely and lightly." (Matthew 11:28-30)

That night I took Jesus' outstretched hand. My hope turned from a feeling I had been lacking to a person I could spend time with.

Gently, God met me as I began to read His Word daily. Slowly, like a new puppy becoming acquainted with its already smitten owners, in His company I realized the amazing love God already had for me. Walking with and watching Him through Scripture, I recovered my life. Hope deferred to future generations became hope realized today.

Bedside prayers for my children shifted from prayers of desperation to abundance. Now, with confidence, as I experience joy and delight in Him, I pray my children and future generations seek and find this love, too.

Jesus is extending the same hope-filled hand to you who, like me, are tired, worn out and doubting God's love when your faith feels distant, lacking or even unobtainable.

God is not withholding. Delight in Him is not beyond your grasp. Jesus is waiting with an outstretched hand, saying:

"I love YOU more than you can comprehend.
I want YOU to love Me more than you think you can.
Spend time with Me."

A Web of Faithfulness

AUBREY CARRALES

"Now may the God of peace, who through the blood of the eternal covenant brought back from the dead our Lord Jesus, that great Shepherd of the sheep, equip you with everything good for doing his will, and may he work in us what is pleasing to him, through Jesus Christ, to whom be glory forever and ever. Amen." Hebrews 13:20-21(NIV)

It had been one of "those" days. I was exhausted from a long day of homeschooling, sibling rivalry and never-ending chores, but I needed to take the trash out to the curb before I went to bed. As I was walking back inside, I spotted a spider on the brick of our house. We had a brief standoff while I made sure it wasn't going to lunge at me or sneak inside. Once I realized the spider was harmless, we both went our separate ways and I quickly forgot about its existence.

I fell into bed, wondering how I'd do it all again tomorrow.

The next morning, I opened our shades to the sight of three huge spider webs on our hydrangeas thanks to last night's spider. The webs were a true work of art — delicate strands of silk connected to each other forming a perfect, beautiful pattern. But perhaps the most amazing part was that the webs were anchored by a long strand of silk to other plants clear across the yard.

God's creation never ceases to amaze me! How did this tiny spider anchor its webs to plants far away and then get over to the hydrangeas to continue its web building? And how does it know to build such beautiful, intricate webs? And to think the spider did all of this work just so it could catch its next meal. What faithfulness!

The book of Hebrews is full of reminders to remain faithful to Jesus. The author encourages us to fix our thoughts on Jesus, (Hebrews 3:1) not to harden our hearts to God's voice, (Hebrews 3:8) to hold firmly to our faith, (Hebrews 4:14) to remain diligent (Hebrews 6:11) and to draw near to God. (Hebrews 10:22) At the end of the book, the author tells us that God will *"... equip you with everything good for doing his will ..."* (Hebrews 13:21).

Let's ponder on that for a few seconds.

God doesn't equip us with only a few good things and then send us on our way, hoping for the best. Instead, He gives us instructions on how to remain faithful to Him, and then He equips us with *"everything good"* for doing what He has created us to do.

Is God calling you to extend extra grace to your kids, to clean up the same mess for the 10th time, to take a meal to a neighbor in need or to accomplish a task that seems impossible? Just as God created the spider with the ability to spin webs and anchor them for stability, God has equipped you with all you need to do His will. Fix your thoughts on Jesus and draw near to Him, and God will equip you to build your own web of faithfulness.

Love Your Way Back to Hope

MELISSA LABIENIEC

"'Love the Lord your God with all your heart and with all your soul and with all your mind.'
This is the first and greatest commandment." Matthew 22:37-38 (NIV)

I couldn't get out of bed. Postpartum depression had hit me hard and it wasn't letting up. In fact, it was only getting worse.

I tried to hide it from all my loved ones, especially those I went to church with. The main thought running constantly through my mind was: *I can't disclose this to them because they won't understand. Imagine if people actually knew what I was struggling with?* For some reason, I was under the impression I wasn't Christian-like, and something was severely wrong. The more I tried, the more I failed. I was in over my head. Way over.

After a while I couldn't keep the act going. While I was absolutely horrified of the truth being revealed, the jig was up. People now knew the real me. The Christian me was dead. I went with it. I had no choice, really. The old saying, "If you can't beat them, join them," resonated like a sad song within me, and I suddenly didn't care to keep hiding it.

Yet I also didn't want to go on in general. It was all too much. Everything was hard.

And I mean everything. At that point in my life, I couldn't even get out of my pajamas.

I wasn't pretending anymore. Though it did feel freeing to let go, it stung that I couldn't be a "normal" Christian like everyone else. I didn't feel like praying.

So I didn't. I didn't feel like going to church. So I didn't. I didn't feel like reading my Bible. So I didn't. I couldn't. Even when I tried, I got frustrated. I was putting on an act to do so. I wanted to want to do those things, but I sincerely had no desire.

One night, it was as if a light switch turned on. Everything changed after my mother-in-law uttered this one simple sentence: "When you cannot give God perfect faith, you can give Him perfect love."

I instantly recalled the words of Jesus: *"'Love the Lord your God with all your heart and with all your soul and with all your mind.' This is the first and greatest commandment"* (Matthew 22:37-38). If I couldn't pray ... if I couldn't read ... if I couldn't go to church ... if everything was too hard ... I could simply love Him. I could do that! I could start there!

At last, I had a reason to go on. It was as if a heavy weight was lifted off my shoulders. The thing was, I did love God. That never changed. Instant comfort resulted from that one life-giving word. Love. All hope was not lost! If I couldn't do anything else, I could just love Him, at least for now. My hope was renewed.

So I loved Him and loved Him and loved Him. I spoke it every chance I got. I loved Him in my every action. I loved Him as much as I could. In return, He loved me back to life!

Hope Is Rising

MISTIE DOYLE

"Jesus Christ is the same yesterday and today and forever." Hebrews 13:8 (NIV)

I keep telling myself nothing about our son has changed. Jack is the same child he was before the diagnosis. The only thing different is a label.

And my heart.

Even though we knew he would land somewhere on the autism spectrum, when the psychologist said it out loud, I wondered how I would carry my heavy heart out of the room. The teacher part of me wanted the diagnosis so he would have the resources and accommodations his special needs warrant. The mother part of me did not want the diagnosis, thinking of the challenges he would face.

Will he ever have a conversation?
Will he have meaningful friendships and relationships?
Will my heart ever stop grieving the future I thought he would have?

The morning of the evaluation, I sent a dear friend a message saying a diagnosis wasn't going to change Jack. He would be the same kid tomorrow as he was today.

She responded: "And God will be the same tomorrow as He is today. The results of this evaluation will be no surprise to Him." Her words brought both conviction and comfort that morning. I had been so focused on Jack's future, I had forgotten that Jesus was already there, waiting with strength and comfort.

God is the same faithful and unchanging God we read about in the Bible. He is still near and has unlimited amounts of peace to offer us on our journeys.

While most days I can rise above the worry and sadness, sometimes I get back on the slope. You know, the slippery one. Where depression fogs your perspective, and things seem worse than they really are. When this happens, I remind myself of Hebrews 13:8 — *"Jesus Christ is the same yesterday and today and forever."* God has never, and will never, run out of the grace I need.

This diagnosis didn't change Jack. It changed me.

I'm learning to dig into God's Word for truth. Then I'm speaking those truths out loud to my heart when it gets caught up in feelings. When I start to feel overwhelmed with worry, I'm resting my mind by listening to worship music or sitting still in His presence.

You can do these same things, friend. When you do, the seeds of hope will sprout, pushing your fog away. And you will trust even more in the God who is already in your tomorrows.

Hope is rising in me. I pray the same for you.

Notes

Notes

Acknowledgments

Proverbs 31 Ministries and COMPEL Training would like to offer a special thanks to the talented devotion writers featured in this book, all of whom are members of COMPEL Training. Their devotions were chosen out of almost 700 submissions in a COMPEL devotion writing challenge. Writers, we congratulate and applaud you for your hard work and dedication to your craft of writing, and for bravely offering your words of truth and encouragement to the world. You are touching hearts and lives in ways you will never understand until eternity. Keep up the good work, faithful servants!

"You are the light of the world. A town built on a hill cannot be hidden. Neither do people light a lamp and put it under a bowl. Instead they put it on its stand, and it gives light to everyone in the house. In the same way, let your light shine before others, that they may see your good deeds and glorify your Father in heaven." (Matthew 5:14-16, NIV)

About Proverbs 31 Ministries

She is clothed with strength and dignity;
she can laugh at the days to come.

PROVERBS 31:25

Proverbs 31 Ministries is a nondenominational, nonprofit Christian ministry that seeks to lead women into a personal relationship with Christ. With Proverbs 31:10-31 as a guide, Proverbs 31 Ministries reaches women in the middle of their busy days through free devotions, podcast episodes, speaking events, conferences, resources, online Bible studies and training in the call to write, speak and lead others.

We are real women offering real-life solutions to those striving to maintain life's balance, in spite of today's hectic pace and cultural pull away from godly principles.

Wherever a woman may be on her spiritual journey, Proverbs 31 Ministries exists to be a trusted friend who understands the challenges she faces and walks by her side, encouraging her as she walks toward the heart of God.

Visit us online today at proverbs31.org!

Proverbs 31
MINISTRIES

Join COMPEL Writers Training

COMPEL WRITERS TRAINING IS A FAITH-BASED
ONLINE WRITERS TRAINING COMMUNITY.

Grow in your calling as a writer by joining COMPEL, where you will:

· Receive insider training from Lysa TerKeurst and other bestselling authors who know the publishing industry inside and out.
· Learn how to overcome the challenges you face as a writer, so you can accomplish your writing goals.
· Gain access to publishing opportunities not found anywhere else, which can help your writing dreams come true.

Whether you are just starting to write or need to figure out your next move, COMPEL can help you identify the next steps and equip you to take them.

LEARN MORE AND SIGN UP FOR JUST $30
A MONTH AT COMPELTRAINING.COM.